Out
of the
Cave

Out of the Cave

STEPPING **INTO THE LIGHT** WHEN
DEPRESSION DARKENS WHAT YOU SEE

CHRIS HODGES

NELSON
BOOKS

An Imprint of Thomas Nelson

Published in Nashville, Tennessee, by Nelson Books, an imprint of Thomas Nelson. Nelson Books and Thomas Nelson are registered trademarks of HarperCollins Christian Publishing, Inc.

Published in association with Yates & Yates, www.yates2.com.

Thomas Nelson titles may be purchased in bulk for educational, business, fundraising, or sales promotional use. For information, please e-mail SpecialMarkets@ThomasNelson.com.

Unless otherwise noted, Scripture quotations taken from The Holy Bible, New International Version®, NIV®. Copyright © 1973, 1978, 1984, 2011 by Biblica, Inc.® Used by permission of Zondervan. All rights reserved worldwide. www.Zondervan.com. The "NIV" and "New International Version" are trademarks registered in the United States Patent and Trademark Office by Biblica, Inc.®

Scripture quotations marked CEB are taken from the Common English Bible. Copyright © 2011 Common English Bible.

Scripture quotations marked ESV are taken from the ESV® Bible (The Holy Bible, English Standard Version®), copyright © 2001 by Crossway, a publishing ministry of Good News Publishers. Used by permission. All rights reserved.

Scripture quotations marked KJV are taken from the King James Version. Public domain.

Scripture quotations marked THE MESSAGE are taken from *THE MESSAGE*. Copyright © 1993, 2002, 2018 by Eugene H. Peterson. Used by permission of NavPress. All rights reserved. Represented by Tyndale House Publishers, Inc.

Scripture quotations marked NKJV are taken from the New King James Version®. Copyright © 1982 by Thomas Nelson. Used by permission. All rights reserved.

Scripture quotations marked NLT are taken from the Holy Bible, New Living Translation. © 1996, 2004, 2015 by Tyndale House Foundation. Used by permission of Tyndale House Publishers, Inc., Carol Stream, Illinois 60188. All rights reserved.

Scripture quotations marked TLB are taken from The Living Bible. Copyright © 1971. Used by permission of Tyndale House Publishers, Inc., Carol Stream, Illinois 60188. All rights reserved.

Library of Congress Cataloging-in-Publication Data

Names: Hodges, Chris (Pastor), author.
Title: Out of the cave : stepping into the light when depression darkens what you see / Chris Hodges.
Description: Nashville, Tennessee : Nelson Books, an imprint of Thomas Nelson, [2021] | Includes bibliographical references. | Summary: "Chris Hodges helps those struggling with depression find liberating solutions by drawing from the life of the prophet Elijah"-- Provided by publisher.
Identifiers: LCCN 2020051548 (print) | LCCN 2020051549 (ebook) | ISBN 9781400221257 (trade paperback) | ISBN 9781400221264 (epub) | ISBN 9781400221288 (audiobook)
Subjects: LCSH: Depressed persons--Religious life. | Depression, Mental--Religious aspects--Christianity. | Christian life.
Classification: LCC BV4910.34 .H64 2021 (print) | LCC BV4910.34 (ebook) | DDC 248.8/61968527--dc23
LC record available at https://lccn.loc.gov/2020051548
LC ebook record available at https://lccn.loc.gov/2020051549

Printed in the United States of America

21 22 23 24 25   LSC   10 9 8 7 6 5 4 3

*This book is dedicated to Rick Bezet. For more than twenty-five years, you have been a faithful and trusted friend.
Our constant conversations always encourage me.
Your positive spirit always lifts me.
You are a gift to me from God.
My prayer is that everyone could have a friend
like you to help them out of the cave.*

Contents

CONTENTS

Foreword

Sometimes you have to experience darkness before you appreciate the light.

I was reminded of this truth during power outages not long ago at home in California. Some blackouts were planned as a measure to prevent the spread of devastating wildfires while others resulted from fluctuating energy supply and increased consumer usage. But regardless of whether we expected electric power to shut down or got caught off guard, we all knew the frustration, discomfort, and inconvenience of finding ourselves in the dark.

Emotional, psychological, and spiritual darkness is even more unsettling. We lose our anchor points and become disoriented, uncertain of which direction leads us forward. Worry and doubt cloud our thinking as fear and anxiety shadow our feelings. Uncertainty, dread, and despair replace the security, joy, and hope we once knew. Worst of all, we often feel powerless to escape our pain and wonder why God feels so far away.

Depression is the word often used to describe our struggles in these times of darkness, usually a catchall for many kinds of mental illness. But identifying the problem doesn't necessarily help us find the solution. Despite the increase of diagnosing and treating depression, the stigma still lingers, even among people of faith. Followers of Jesus, however, should be first responders to those battling the darkness of depression. We should be compassionate facilitators of hope and healing, following the example set by Christ during his time on earth. The church should be a primary resource for eradicating the stigma and serving those in need of treatment.

We've stigmatized mental illness and depression for far too long. It's not a sin to be sick, and your character isn't defined by your chemistry. Your identity is not based on your illness. Your brain, like your heart or lungs, is just another organ in your body. Christians can suffer depression and mental illness just like they experience a toothache, broken bone, or clogged artery, just as any human being does. When our physical health breaks down, we seek treatment, take medication as prescribed, and pursue recovery.

Similarly, when our mental and emotional health causes suffering, we must not ignore it, deny it, or shame ourselves for what we experience. Instead, we see medical professionals, take medication if needed, and face causes and contributors we can modify or change. We work with doctors, counselors, therapists, pastors, and other believers to restore our minds just as we would our bodies. We pursue holistic healing so we can experience the fullness of life God created us to enjoy, the same fullness fueling our ministry to those around us. Rather than hide our struggles to regain mental health, we can find support, strength, and hope by honestly sharing our battles.

Which is why I'm grateful my friend Chris Hodges has written *Out of the Cave*. I've admired and respected Chris since he started Church of the Highlands two decades ago. Right out of the gate, his leadership impressed me and his faith inspired me. God had clearly given Chris a vision for creating and sustaining a thriving, purpose driven church, and Chris listened and obeyed.

I've also appreciated the personal connection Chris brings to his insightful teaching of God's Word, and this book reflects the best of both. As leaders, we must be honest about our own mental health challenges. We're just as human as anyone else, and our struggles are just as painful. Becoming a leader doesn't insulate us from depression and anxiety, and Chris has battled them just as I have. He's also discovered that we must never give up in those seasons of struggle but persevere through them, moment by moment and hour by hour, trusting God to guide us forward. And those painful battles are never wasted.

I'm a firm believer that your greatest ministry always flows out of your greatest pain. During the times when I've felt lost in a cave of depression, God never gave up on me and repeatedly met me there and brought me back into the light of his truth. I remember feeling depressed for most of my second year as pastor of Saddleback Church. But God not only sustained me but used that experience as a catalyst for some of the most significant developments of my ministry there.

God never wastes our pain, and followers of Jesus should never shy away from showing people this truth in the context of our lives. When we begin to show our own frailty, we also reveal God's power to bring hope, to restore health, and to redeem suffering. This is the gift Chris gives us throughout these pages. He not only shares his own struggles openly and honestly, but he also guides us alongside the prophet Elijah's journey.

The result is a resource shining the truth of God's Word into your life along with the encouragement of a caring brother. Chris is upfront about his limitations as an expert on depression and mental illness, but I believe he underestimates his wisdom and expertise in treating our souls. He knows what it means to wrestle with the kind of overwhelming emotions that often sideline us. He has walked through the valley of the shadow of loss and felt the deep ache of sorrow and grief.

More importantly, though, Chris has heard the whisper of God's Spirit inviting him, reviving him, empowering him. The same invitation Elijah received thousands of years ago in the utter darkness of his own fears, disappointments, and exhaustion. The same opportunity you have right now as well.

Because if you look for him, God will meet you in these pages. Right where you are. The psalmist says, "The righteous cry out, and the LORD hears them; he delivers them from all their troubles. The LORD is close to the brokenhearted and saves those who are crushed in spirit" (Psalm 34:17–18 NIV). Whether you're struggling with depression or hoping to serve and encourage others in the battle, *Out of the Cave* separates science from stigma, fact from fiction, and instructs as much as it encourages.

So consider this book a match to ignite your faith again, a spark to kindle hope in the power of God in your life. Don't let the stigma and shame of your suffering leave you wandering in the dark. Because you don't have to stay there. There's never a shortage or outage with God's power. If you seek him where you are, God will meet you there. It's time to come out of your cave and into his light!

Rick Warren
Founding Pastor, Saddleback Church
Author, *The Purpose Driven Life*

Introduction

An Invitation to Come Out of Your Cave

*P*astor's Suicide Leaves Many Heartbroken

The headline jumped from my phone screen and cut right through me.

Although I had never met him, I knew his name and was aware we had friends and acquaintances in common. The news of anyone's suicide saddens me, but when I read about this pastor's decision to take his own life, I was devastated—for him, his wife and children, his church family, his friends and community. I recalled two other pastors who had made the same tragic choice in the past couple of years, but somehow this latest loss felt more personal.

I could identify with the intense pressure of juggling the many demands of leading a church and shepherding the people entrusted to your care. Often invisible to others, the toll of being in full-time vocational ministry can leave a pastor weary and wounded, vulnerable to burnout and self-sabotage. As a pastor to other pastors, I also knew that even when you have the hope of heaven, the pain on earth can weigh too heavily. The darkness of depression is real even when you're living in the light of God's grace.

Pastors, along with all followers of Jesus, are not immune from depression.

I've experienced my own battles with depression, but news of this latest suicide prompted me to investigate further, to search for the latest findings on depression's causes, and more importantly, to explore viable solutions. The prospect intimidated me because I'm a pastor, not a doctor. I knew that in addition to Bible study, understanding more about depression would require a deep dive into psychology, neurology, biology, sociology, and various other fields of study.

But I also knew this couldn't keep happening. I had to do something. This latest pastor's suicide opened my eyes. Depression seemed to be gaining ground, even among Christians, and it was time to fight back.

Because I believe what Jesus said is true: "I have come into the world as a light, so that no one who believes in me should stay in darkness" (John 12:46).

Bad News and Good News About Depression

As I began my research on depression, many sources confirmed the bad news: It has become the world's number one health problem, causing more deaths than cancer each year and ranking as the leading cause of disability.[1] In fact, one out of every nine people are on some type of depression-treating medication, and one out of every five people have been at some point. Over the past decade, anti-depressant use has gone up 300 percent and it continues to increase.[2]

But there's also good news: More and more research indicates we need to rethink some of our assumptions about depression. We may have more control over variables leading to depression than we realize. There's a strong chance that what we often call the symptoms of depression come from areas of our lives in need of our attention rather than the disease itself. Conditioning from our culture and choices about how we live contribute to a host of symptoms, illnesses, and conditions falling under the mental health umbrella of depression. The latest studies, many of which are cited throughout this book, reveal many of the daily choices we make may be setting us up to be depressed.

Whatever the causes and contributing factors, one thing is certain: depression and anxiety spill into the lives of more people every year. You've probably already heard this news and, more likely, have met depression face-to-face. And if you haven't squared off against depression personally, chances are you've seen it in the life of a loved one, family member, or close friend.

No matter who we are, where we live, or what we do for a living, no matter our level of education or income, our ethnicity or gender, it's possible we'll struggle with depression at some point. Depression doesn't discriminate. Depression chokes us of pleasure, purpose, joy, peace, happiness, and contentment. It clouds our vision, sometimes quickly but often gradually, and prevents us from seeing ourselves, our lives, and God clearly.

In my own journey, I've struggled with several serious bouts of depression and anxiety. And just like so many other people, I've received medical advice and have been offered prescriptions from well-intentioned doctors focused on helping me cope. Their recommendations may have helped me in the short term, but I suspected that defeating depression in the long haul required more than just the benefits of medication.

Please understand that I'm not underestimating the difference the right prescription can make. I've seen it firsthand in the life of my son, diagnosed at a young age on the autism spectrum. He has a chemical imbalance that makes his life difficult, and several years ago, he told my wife and me that his torment was so overwhelming he wanted to die. We quickly did everything in our power to help him find relief from his suffering. We remain grateful that the expertise of his doctors and the medications they prescribed diminished his pain and made my son's life bearable again—and saved his life.

And yet, medication alone can't address an even greater need in his life—the need for purpose. My son, like each of us, wasn't created to merely survive but to *thrive*—to be productive, to make a difference, to experience the fulfillment that comes from doing what he is meant to do in this life. The same is true for you and me—we all need purpose.

I share these personal disclosures because I want you to know from the start that I would never discount what doctors do and advise. They are much needed, and I continue to turn to them, like most of us do, for solutions to a vast spectrum of health issues. But, again, I also recognize that medication alone is not enough when it comes to depression. Even as drug use, both prescription and recreational, continues to rise, many problems—depression in particular—aren't getting better.

There is clearly a need for something else. We must have higher goals than just alleviating the pain. Because for many of us, the underlying pain is still there. We receive treatments for one issue or another, often taking additional meds to address side effects of primary medications. Yet we still feel like our lives are falling apart and wonder if healing is even possible.

Why is this happening to us?

Why do more and more of us find it harder to simply get through the day?

Why do we worry about the future and carry the pain of the past instead of engaging in the present?

How do we fight this thing?

Better yet, how do we win the battle?

Spiritual Solutions

Once I started looking closer at the causes of depression and anxiety, searching for lasting solutions beyond medication, my investigation brought me back to God's Word. Yes, I always believe the answers to any and every problem are within its pages. To be clear, I'm not saying that every solution is simply reciting a Bible verse or passively waiting around and trusting God to drop a remedy in your lap, particularly when dealing with depression and anxiety.

But I do believe we are fundamentally spiritual beings in physical bodies who are created in the image of God. That means we need spiritual solutions as well as medical solutions. I believe there is healing wisdom and power in the Word of God. As a pastor, I haven't been trained to address the physical aspects of depression, but I am equipped to guide you in seeking solutions for your spiritual health. And as I see it, your spiritual health affects all parts of your being, including the physical, emotional, and mental.

So I went to God's Word looking for solutions to depression and found an amazing story about a prophet named Elijah. He experienced the highest of highs and the lowest of lows—sometimes one right after the other. In fact, after one of his greatest spiritual victories, Elijah wanted to give up and take his own life. He ran away, isolated himself, and hid in a dark cave.

Can you relate?

But God met Elijah right where he was. Rather than rebuke the prophet, the Lord invited Elijah to step forward, leave his cave, and embark on a divinely appointed mission. With a renewed sense of purpose, the prophet then became a mentor for a younger man named Elisha, and together God used them to change the world.

In Elijah's story, I saw several causes for his depression that I recognized and found relatable. Even more exciting, I also discovered relevant and practical solutions to address the underlying spiritual issues so many of us struggle with while battling depression. I'm convinced tracing the prophet's journey reveals a way forward and out of the cave of depression. Elijah's story will serve as our metaphoric flashlight, and you'll see it again and again throughout these pages, along with my most important research findings and personal stories, to help you find your own way forward.

There are no easy answers here, but you may be startled by Elijah's raw honesty and God's tender mercies. God met Elijah in the midst of his depression and provided for his needs—physically, emotionally, and spiritually.

Fighting for Control

Before we enter Elijah's story, however, we must consider a more foundational starting point—one that shows us how our spiritual life significantly influences our emotional and physical health. We are triune beings, with bodies, souls, and spirits. The body is our visible form. The soul consists of our mind, our will, and our emotions. The spirit reflects how we are made in God's image and is the part of us that will live forever. Each of these three aspects of our being has its own needs and desires, and each continually wrestles the other two for control of our lives.

When your body is in control, your priority is satisfying physical needs and cravings based on what makes the body feel good. With the body in charge, you eat what you want when you want, and you make decisions based on how they affect you physically (toward pleasure and away from pain), often with little regard for how those decisions affect the rest of you (soul and spirit). Basically the body says, if it feels good, do it!

When your soul is in charge, priorities shift to whatever you value most—approval, achievement, beauty, celebrity, power, wealth, control. For example, if your soul calls the shots and knows that being thin and attractive will get you the attention and affection that means so much to you, then it will override what your body needs in order to be thin and attractive.

When the spirit is in charge, the priority is achieving a life of peace in God's presence. Your spirit is what keeps body and soul connected and in check. When your spirit is in charge, the needs of both body and soul are given their due, but they no longer battle for dominance. The apostle Paul wrote:

> Those who live according to the flesh [body and soul] have their minds set on what the flesh desires; but those who live in accordance with the Spirit have their minds set on what the Spirit desires. The mind governed by the flesh [body and soul] is death, but the mind governed by the Spirit is *life and peace.* (Romans 8:5–6, emphasis added)

So how do we become governed by the Spirit?

We surrender body and soul.

If we want to overcome depression, we have to strengthen our spirits and allow God's Spirit to empower us and lead the way. We have to let our spirits follow Jesus' example so our bodies and souls align with God's instructions and guidelines for living.

Please do attend to the causes and conditions of depression in your body and in your soul. Seek help from medical doctors and professional counselors. But don't neglect your spirit in the process. Focus on strengthening your faith and growing spiritually while also addressing other causes holistically. When your spirit grows stronger, it will benefit your body and soul as well.

Depression is a multidimensional problem that requires a multidimensional solution. The invitation of this book is to allow God's Spirit to lead your spirit as you also care for body and soul. God helped Elijah restore balance in his body and soul and get his spirit back in working order. *God will do the same for you—if you let him.*

If you're struggling with depression and losing the battle, maybe you're going about it in the wrong way. What if what you need most is a fresh, intimate encounter with the living God? What would happen if you listened for the whisper of his Spirit and stepped forward out of the darkness around you?

It's time to get your life back.

It's time to stop pretending that Christians don't get depressed.

It's time to get real with God about where you are and who's in charge.

It's time to step forward into his light and enjoy the life he has for you.

It's time to come out of your cave.

PART 1

Defining Depression

CHAPTER 1

Just Like Us

Elijah was a person just like us.
JAMES 5:17 (CEB)

I don't know how I got here.

Worse yet, I don't know how to get out from underneath this heaviness that is swallowing me whole. I'm alive but not tuned in to my life. I'm stuck in a fishbowl, looking out at all I should be so happy about and grateful for, but I can't break through to feel or enjoy any of it.

Seeing my life but not being able to truly participate in it is maddening, but I'm too exhausted to do much about it. Just getting out of bed in the morning feels like an epic accomplishment. It's so exhausting that I just want to crawl back between the sheets, pull the covers over my head, and will the world to go away. It's already moving on without me anyway. The world loves people who contribute, who are productive and efficient, and who remain cheerfully positive no matter what. Right now, I'm none of those things. Was I ever any of them to begin with? Will I ever be again? What is my life worth if I feel utterly unable to live it?

The dark fog nips at the edges of my soul. And I fear that one day, every bit of light inside me will disappear. Darkness will just swallow me up.

A Mystery with No Clues

This is how I've felt sometimes.

Many people may think of me as some great pastor, but when it comes to depression, I battle it along with millions of other people. Just like you do, I'm guessing.

These feelings summed up my life back in 1999, for sure. There was no one, overriding cause or crisis that precipitated my depression. Just a slow, cumulative, creeping sense of losing touch with my life. And at the time, it made no sense.

As a husband to an amazing wife and a father to a growing number of little kids, I always felt guilty for not feeling happier. I loved my wife and she loved me. We had been blessed with healthy children who brightened our busy lives. But something felt just a little off-kilter inside me.

I often felt like I didn't measure up and couldn't provide what my kids needed. I knew I should be reading stories, helping with homework, and playing hide-and-seek, but many times I didn't have the energy to even try. I knew what I wanted to do—what I thought I should do— but I couldn't muster the willpower to do it. This left me feeling like a failure—a fitting bow on top of the empty package of my intentions.

Life at work wasn't much different. My coworkers and other staff members seemed genuinely happy and fully engaged with their lives and the many people we served at our church and in the community. I can remember sitting in the middle of a team meeting and feeling lost—there but not *there*, not engaged.

At the end of the workday, I'd head home and find myself driving on autopilot. When I suddenly realized I was almost home, I'd turn for no reason, taking a longer route without understanding why I was prolonging my commute.

Once I did manage to find my way home, I still felt like I was going through the motions. I talked to Tammy, asked the kids about their day, and ate dinner with the family. On weekends, I prepared for Sunday services, especially if I was preaching, but I didn't look forward to being at church no matter how much I tried. Sunday nights, I crashed as the adrenaline from the day's activities wore off. I tried to relax but couldn't. The best I could manage was to dive into a bowl of ice cream or tube of chocolate chip cookie dough while watching something on television that everyone else seemed to find entertaining.

I felt like a mystery to myself, a mere bystander in my own life. Part of me was always detached, an observer of my invisible suffering. I tried to lift the weight crushing down on me, but it felt like trying to solve a problem I couldn't yet identify. I was afraid to find out what was really going on below the surface. Afraid I didn't have what it took to look my depression in the eye and win.

When Pushing Through Is Pulling You Apart

Some people seem to be especially susceptible to depression. Some of us try to fake our way through it in hopes it will go away. But that just doesn't work, and inevitably it'll creep back into our lives. Some roles, seasons, and situations, for example, naturally set us up to experience stress, pressure, and more anxiety than we're used to facing. We get married or become new parents, move to a new home or a new state, start a new job or get promoted at our current one. These should all be happy milestones, right? So why do we feel so heavy, so burdened, so overwhelmed sometimes when they happen? It can be confusing and can tempt us to push away these more negative feelings when they pop up.

It's incredibly dangerous, though, to ignore the ways depression advances. Telling yourself you're too busy or too strong or too spiritual to be depressed won't stop the internal skirmishes from escalating into a daily battle or prevent the grinding battles from gaining ground in the bigger war on your soul. Pushing through will only get you so far. And then you get stuck. And when that happens, the daily battles you once pushed through will begin to pull you apart. Ask me how I know.

But I also know this—you and I can win these daily battles and claim victory in the war.

You don't have to lose touch with the light when the dark cave of depression tries to swallow you. When pushing through is pulling you apart, you can find rest. While there is no easy three-step solution, there are practical strategies for helping yourself, accepting God's help, and reaching out to others. In fact, once you get the help you need, you'll be able to extend the same lifeline to others.

In these pages, I promise to share my own hardest-fought and most painful battles. I will not sugarcoat the jagged, raw reality of depression. But I am also eager to share my victories; none came easily but all were that much sweeter for the struggle. We'll look at different aspects of the causes of and contributors to depression and then focus on a manageable, step-by-step approach to care for your body, your soul, and your spirit.

Look Who's Here

Before I share more of my battles with depression, let me introduce you to one of the truly great people in the Bible. He's considered, both in ancient times and present day, to be one of the greatest prophets and most powerful miracle workers in history. And although he lived several hundred years before Christ, Elijah makes an appearance at one of the seminal events of Jesus' ministry, usually called the transfiguration (Matthew 17:1–8; Mark 9:2–8; Luke 9:28–36; 2 Peter 1:16–18).

When Jesus' earthly ministry was concluding, his body experienced a metamorphosis into pure light and shone like the sun. Christ had verified that he was the Messiah and predicted his imminent death and resurrection. The disciples who witnessed the transfiguration of Jesus also saw Moses and Elijah with him. Their appearance at this event is highly significant. Moses represented the Old Testament law that God had given to the people. Jesus came and fulfilled the commandments of the law and did the things the law could not do, that is, provide an answer for the problem of sin. The law pointed out the problem; Jesus gave the solution: "For the law was given through Moses; grace and truth came through Jesus Christ" (John 1:17).

Elijah, an outstanding prophet in the Old Testament, testified that Jesus had not only fulfilled the law of Moses but all the prophets. Many people believe Elijah is one of the two witnesses at the end of time mentioned in Revelation 11:3–12. Although he is not named, evidence supports this inference. Either way, Elijah remains a figure of exceptional importance.

During his earthly ministry as God's prophet, Elijah performed many miracles and received many blessings. For example, he caused the rain to cease for more than three years (1 Kings 17:1), brought a widow's son back to life (1 Kings 17:22), and parted the Jordan River (2 Kings 2:8). Elijah also was fed by ravens (1 Kings 17:4), called fire from heaven to burn an altar drenched in water three times (1 Kings 18:38), and mentored his successor, Elisha (2 Kings 2). Clearly, Elijah was someone who knew God well and served him with dedication, authority, and heavenly power.

With all those connections to God and all that affirmation from heaven, we might think Elijah never struggled in his faith. But you know what? He not only struggled to trust God, Elijah got so depressed that he wanted to die.

That makes him someone I want to know more about.

Someone we can all learn from.

Someone just like us, who faced the same kind of depression you and I battle.

And who somehow won.

Fired Up

As God's chosen prophet to deliver his message to the people of Israel, Elijah warned the Israelites of impending doom if they continued to reject God. Numerous miracles verified the divine authenticity of Elijah's message, but one stands out above the others. His most famous display of God's power involved a showdown with King Ahab and the prophets of a false god named Baal. When Ahab labeled the prophet a troublemaker, Elijah rebuked Israel's king. "'I have not made trouble for Israel,' Elijah replied. 'But you and your father's family have. You have abandoned the LORD's commands and have followed the Baals'" (1 Kings 18:18).

To break their stalemate, Elijah proposed a decisive test to reveal the one true and living God: each would prepare a bull for burnt offering but not light it, praying instead for divine ignition. The altar catching fire would demonstrate the power of the living God (vv. 22–24). The 450 prophets of Baal got right to work. They prayed from morning until midday, but nothing happened. Elijah taunted them, saying, "Shout louder! . . . Perhaps [Baal] is deep in thought, or busy, or traveling. Maybe he is sleeping and must be awakened"

(v. 27). So the prophets took things up several notches in the afternoon, shouting louder and even slashing themselves "until their blood flowed" to prove their devotion (v. 28). Still, nothing.

Then it was Elijah's turn. The prophet chose twelve stones, one for each tribe of Israel, and built an altar. He dug a trench around the altar and arranged wood on top of it to burn the slaughtered bull. He then asked onlookers to fill four large jars with water and drench the bull and the wood—not just once but *three* times! Elijah prayed fervently and got an immediate response: "Then the fire of the LORD fell and burned up the sacrifice, the wood, the stones and the soil, and also licked up the water in the trench" (v. 38). Talk about a mic-drop moment!

When the crowd saw what had happened, they fell on their faces and cried, "The LORD—he is God! The LORD—he is God!" (v. 39). And then, to put a fine point on God's victory, Elijah commanded the people to seize Baal's prophets, and all 450 were slaughtered that day.

King Ahab was not only humiliated but also outraged by Elijah's decisive victory. Needless to say, he and his equally wicked queen, Jezebel, were not motivated to repent:

> Now Ahab told Jezebel everything Elijah had done and how he had killed all the prophets with the sword. So Jezebel sent a messenger to Elijah to say, "May the gods deal with me, be it ever so severely, if by this time tomorrow I do not make your life like that of one of them." (1 Kings 19:1–2)

Given the stunning success of the showdown at Mount Carmel, we might expect Jezebel's threat to bounce right off Elijah. No one who witnessed fire fall from heaven that day could doubt that God was clearly in his corner. And yet, he immediately fell apart.

Elijah was afraid and ran for his life. When he came to Beersheba in Judah, he left his servant there, while he himself went a day's journey into the wilderness. He came to a broom bush, sat down under it and prayed that he might die. "I have had enough, LORD," he said. "Take my life; I am no better than my ancestors." (vv. 3–4)

After facilitating one of the greatest, most dramatic displays of divine power in Israel's history, Elijah collapsed in terror at the threat of an adversary he had just defeated. Seemingly in a matter of hours, if not minutes, he went from the heights of prophetic confidence to the depths of suicidal despair. What happened? What shifted within him that would cause him to doubt God's power and protection, especially in the wake of such a spiritual triumph?

The answer is simple, really. *What goes up, often comes down.* After getting all fired up, it was almost inevitable that Elijah would cave in.

Caving In

You see, depression often comes on the heels of a spiritual and emotional high. When we reach a milestone, attain a goal, or receive God's long-awaited answer to our prayers, we experience exhilaration, excitement, and joy. But we can only sustain this level of high-octane energy for so long, and then our emotions have nowhere to go but down.

Early on in ministry, I noticed that Sunday nights were the lowest part of every week for me. While I often felt relieved, grateful, and fulfilled at how well our church services had gone that day, I also experienced an intense emptiness. I was physically exhausted and emotionally depleted, and my spirit usually followed suit; I wasn't sure how to prevent the downward slide into depression. My defenses felt weak and often unable to resist the temptation of numbing myself with junk food and mindless TV.

Ironically, while I felt what I was doing was mindless, my mind was definitely at work, creating a distressing narrative. In fact, depression often comes when the mind subtly takes over. In my case, that took the form of obsessing about my performance—specifically, that week's sermon—and going over what I wish I had done differently. I ruminated endlessly on each facet and judged myself more harshly than anyone else would judge me. I compared how I thought it went with the perfect and unrealistic ideal I used as my standard. Which meant I constantly felt like I was missing the mark.

When I wasn't obsessing about the past, I was fixated on the future and feeling overwhelmed. I worried about what might go wrong, who might be upset, or when the other shoe might drop. I compared myself to other people and resented their happiness in light of the burdens I was carrying. When I looked ahead, all I could see was what I lacked and how inadequate I felt. Like so many others who struggle with depression, I often thought if only I had those missing pieces—whatever I believed would make me happy and successful—I would finally be content.

But enough is rarely enough. And I'm guessing this dynamic played at least some part in Elijah's dramatic downfall.

The prophet had been fearless for three long years, culminating in an amazing victory. Yet it only took one threat and he instantly caved and cowered in fear. He turned and ran away to the edge of the desert where depression enveloped him. He hid under a tree until God sent an angel who nourished Elijah with bread and water (1 Kings 19:5–8). "Strengthened by that food, he traveled forty days and forty nights until he reached Horeb, the mountain of God. There he went into a cave and spent the night" (vv. 8–9).

Now, if you've ever been spelunking, you know how disorienting the inside of a cave can be. You can't see in the vast ebony ocean of darkness. Sounds echo and reverberate indirectly. Dank, earthy smells permeate the chilly air. Creatures may go skittering or flapping, felt but unseen. In other words, even when it provides shelter from dangers outside, a cave can be scary and unfamiliar inside—which makes it an especially apt metaphor for depression.

To enter the cave of depression is to retreat alone into darkness. You may feel safer temporarily, but you're also all alone. You've lost your direction. You can't trust your senses and the usual data they provide to help you navigate your surroundings. It isn't long until you're afraid you may never find your way back out.

That's depression. It pulls you into complete darkness, utter aloneness, total disorientation, and sensory distortion.

That's where Elijah found himself.

But with God's help, he also found his way out.

So can you.

God in the Dark

Like you and me and the millions of others who experience depression, Elijah wanted to give up. But he didn't. Instead, God met him where he was by sending an angel to give him sustenance so he could continue his journey and discover all God had for him. God's presence came, and Elijah was touched by God.

His powerlessness met the God of all power.

His feeling of a future in question met the God who controls all the answers.

His fearful hiding place became a meeting place with the God who is everywhere.

Whatever you're going through right now, trust that God will meet you there. It may be that you're seeking insight about a past season of dwelling in a cave of depression. You're not there now, but you fear you could fall into it again. Or maybe you can't imagine ever slipping into such a hopeless, desperate pit—and I pray you never do—but you know plenty of friends or loved ones who fight an ongoing battle with depression. You wish you knew how to help them, how to pray for them, and how to love them in the midst of their struggles.

You might be hunkered down in a cold, dark cave of depression right now. Your life has lost purpose, meaning, and joy. You go through the motions but feel numb, detached, watching yourself from a distance. The lonely ache of weary, soul-crushing pain gnaws at your bones. Food has no taste. You rarely sleep. You don't know how you got here or what to do to reclaim your life.

No matter where you are, I invite you to believe that this is the beginning of something new—a true breakthrough.

Just as Elijah did, you can discover fresh hope, new life, deep peace, abiding joy, and can't-wait-to-face-the-day purpose. Such possibilities may feel out of reach right now, but taking that first step out of your cave will lead you to discover these key truths:

- God knows what you're going through, and he loves you. He wants to give you freedom, blessings, influence, anointing, and protection.
- God knows your thoughts, and he promises to renew your mind as you learn how to take those thoughts captive and make them obedient to Christ.
- God knows your weaknesses, and he promises to give you strength right in the midst of them. Christ in you is stronger than the depression, anxiety, and fear in you.
- God knows your gifts, and he has a unique assignment for you. You can wake up with purpose, direction, and meaning every

day of your life. The world will be different and better because you showed others Jesus by who you are, what you do, and what you say.

Yes, you may be in a cave right now.

So was I. So was Elijah. So were countless others.

But God will meet you there. His light shines through the darkness, and freedom is closer than you think.

Just take the next step.

Turn the page.

And let's take the journey together—into the light.

CHAPTER 2

What You Might Not Know
About Depression

Depression is the inability to construct a future.
—Rollo May

If someone asked you to post a definition of depression by describing what it feels like, what would you say? As it turns out, there's actually a hashtag for that, #depressionfeelslike, and here's what some people have said.

Depression feels like:

You've lost something but have no clue when or where you had it.
A terrible sinking sensation.
Missing my friends but not having the energy to interact with them.
A void that sucks in all your thoughts of being capable, worthwhile, and loveable, and replaces them with a crushing fear of failure.
Walking around in a big bubble of tar.
You're stuck in quicksand slowly drowning, but only enough to see the world doing just fine without you.

Being scared all the time.

Losing who you are because you've been pretending to be okay for so
long that you can't remember what you're like beneath the mask.[1]

Perhaps you can relate.

Depression has become such a common experience that it might seem like everyone knows what it is, especially since so many of us know what it feels like. And yet it can be difficult to understand by its symptoms and manifestations alone. Even when we suffer from depression, there are many things we might not know about it, including the emotional, biological, and social factors that trigger it.

Guess That's Why They Call It the Blues

You've probably heard someone say, "I'm feeling kind of blue today." Or maybe you've even said something similar yourself to express feelings of depression. People have long referred to experiencing depression as having "the blues," although no one seems to know the origin of this colloquial expression. Nonetheless, the color blue holds a longstanding association with feelings of sadness, loss, grief, and heartache.

Some research has pointed to this phrase being tied to maritime history, perhaps from the seventeenth or eighteenth century.[2] During long voyages ships would sometimes sail off course and lose familiar bearings, typically because the ship's captain had died. Nearing an unknown or unscheduled port, sailors would raise a blue flag or paint a blue band along their vessel's hull to signal to those on shore that they had lost their captain and their way. They didn't want to be mistaken as pirates or hostile invaders and fired upon when they were merely off course. If this is indeed the origin of the phrase, I'm struck by the fact that it refers to feeling out of sorts and lost first, which, in turn, naturally leads to fear and distress.

Other sources mention a reference made by the great nineteenth-century naturalist and artist John James Audubon in his journal. In one entry in 1827 Audubon mentions that he "had the blues."[3] A few decades later, a new musical genre known as the blues originated in the South. Started by slaves, former slaves, and newly emancipated African Americans, the blues incorporated African musical traditions along with spirituals and work songs. "Singing the blues" became a way to express the misery, loss, hurt, and misfortune its singers and songwriters felt.

Whatever the origins—whether "feeling blue" came from seventeenth-century sailors or nineteenth-century former slaves—we know the struggle with feeling lost and deeply out of sorts has been around for a long time. And despite being the number one health problem in the world today, depression carries a stigma we can't seem to shake. Many of us still seem reluctant to admit our struggle with depression, concerned others might think us weak, too sensitive, or undisciplined. We're conditioned to believe that if we have our lives together, we won't experience depression—especially if we're followers of Jesus who live by faith and obey God's Word.

But depression is real. It's just as real as cancer, multiple sclerosis, diabetes, heart disease, and arthritis. Mental illness is just as real and debilitating as any physical illness or injury. The causes may be harder to pinpoint and the symptoms harder to treat than some physical diseases, but this only makes depression more powerful in its subtlety. Many people recognize their depression only after it has robbed them of what once gave their lives pleasure, passion, and purpose. The word *anhedonia*, which means the inability to experience enjoyment from previously favored activities, is derived from a Greek word that translates literally as "without pleasure." People suffering from this symptom of depression may lose interest in hobbies, exercise, music, church, food, travel, work, relationships, and sex.

Recently, mental health experts have expanded the definition of anhedonia to include losing even the *motivation* for enjoyable pursuits as well as the actual fulfillment derived from engaging in the activity itself. I think this could explain why so many of us default to spending time online rather than engaging our real life circumstances and relationships. Why wrestle with the complex problems of day-to-day life when it's so much easier to battle video game enemies you can quickly identify and shoot? Why do the hard and messy work of loving your friends, family, and coworkers when you can have commitment-free relationships through role-playing games, social media, or online porn?

Another thing that makes the virtual world so appealing is the level of control you have, especially when depression leaves you feeling so out of control. You can hide as much as you want about yourself. You don't have to look anyone in the eye. You can control your image or avatar. You can escape your pain by becoming someone totally different, someone who is unencumbered by the depression swirling within the real you.

Whether it's the virtual world, substance abuse, or any number of other escapist tactics, our attempts to deal with depression almost inevitably cause us to avoid experiencing life in the direct, pure ways God intended. No wonder so many of us are depressed! There's so much we're avoiding and so much pain to process that we are desperate to put off dealing with it. But denying or postponing depression only drives it deeper by masking the symptoms and temporarily numbing the pain.

In order to overcome depression, we have to call it what it is and deal with it directly. To do that, it's helpful to understand the variety of factors that cause or contribute to becoming depressed in the first place. These include emotional triggers for depression as well as biological and social factors.

Emotional Triggers for Depression

While emotional triggers for depression vary, some have universal human resonance. Let's go over just a few of them.

GRIEF

When we experience loss, we naturally grieve. The Bible confirms this process: "Be merciful to me, LORD, for I am in distress; my eyes grow weak with sorrow, my soul and body with grief" (Psalm 31:9). Consider what people around the world experienced during the COVID-19 pandemic. Most of us felt what experts call "ambiguous grief" as we lost not only jobs, income, or even loved ones, but less-concrete, easy-to-identify things like a virus-free mind-set and our previous lifestyle. For some, this developed into chronic mourning because their lives would never be the same again.

LEARNED HELPLESSNESS

Grief often flows into another trigger for depression, which is a sense of learned helplessness. When events happen beyond our control, we feel powerless and untethered from our previous reality. Because we can't do what we used to do, we lose sight of the options that still remain within our ability to choose. Our minds create a false narrative, often based on imagining worst-case scenarios, that leaves us feeling like helpless, hopeless victims. We then draw erroneous conclusions that our helpless condition is personal, pervasive, and permanent.

DISAPPOINTMENT

Even if we don't feel powerless, disappointment and unfulfilled expectations can also trigger depression. I recall times when ministry goals went unmet, often for justifiable and sound reasons, but I still felt let down after holding such high expectations. When we assume things will go one way and they go another, we question ourselves and the world around us. We often choose to believe these events would have turned out differently if we had made other, better choices, but this is only an attempt to prop up a false sense of control. It's easier to believe we're not measuring up in some way than to accept that life is often unpredictable and full of painful twists and turns.

Loss of Purpose

Any experience that leads us to believe we're unneeded, irrelevant, or unwanted can lead to depression. When we're not able to use our gifts or make the contribution God designed us to share with the world, we feel inferior, perhaps even invisible. We lose sight of the eternal impact we're intended to have in this life and then settle for distracting ourselves with striving after what we falsely believe can make us happy—money, relationships, sex, fame, or whatever.

Biological and Social Factors in Depression

In addition to emotional triggers, depression also results from a combination of biological and social factors. Doctors, scientists, psychologists, and neurologists agree that depression is rarely the result of a single factor. Instead, it is a complex collection of layered variables, including genetic tendencies, vulnerability due to disease and injury, life circumstances and stressful events, and medications. A change or disruption in any of these areas can cause a domino effect that topples us into depression yet again.

The individualized nature of what causes depression explains why it can be so challenging to find treatments and solutions that work effectively for the majority of people—what helps one person may or may not help another. Nonetheless, because depression has emerged as such a pervasive problem for millions of people world-wide, thousands of studies have been conducted to identify causes, preventions, and treatments. Many studies focus on the biological and physiological causes and contributors to depression, often called *endogenous depression*, while others focus on the external circumstances and traumatic life events contributing to its onset, known as *reactive depression*.

Ultimately, I'm concerned with the spiritual aspects of depression, which I believe affect us all in ways more similar than other variables. That's because our spiritual beliefs, practices, and outlooks have a direct connection to every other area of life. So, again, even though my overall focus is to provide a spiritual and biblical perspective on depression, I believe that includes looking at depression holistically. I want to be clear and consistent in respecting all other factors, particularly those that are biological.

Biological Factors

Most doctors agree that citing a "chemical imbalance" as the cause of depression is too simplistic. Why? Mostly because many chemicals are involved, both in the brain and throughout the body. Researchers at Harvard write, "There are millions, even billions, of chemical reactions that make up the dynamic system that is responsible for your mood, perceptions, and how you experience life."[4]

A change in any one of these chemicals can cause a chain reaction throughout the entire body, especially in the healthy functioning of neurotransmitters, the chemical conduits that transmit messages from nerve cells to various other target cells, such as those in muscles, organs, and glands. Neurotransmitters include chemicals, such as serotonin, norepinephrine, and dopamine—all very important to the body's healthy functioning and how it reacts to problems, conflicts, stress, and danger. It makes sense then how every bodily system can be derailed from healthy functioning when there's too much or, more likely, not enough of certain neurotransmitters.

Neurotransmitters often adversely affect the unique ways particular areas of our brains work. For example, the hippocampus is a small, curved part of the limbic system that's tucked into the central interior of our brain's temporal lobe. The hippocampus interfaces with other parts of our brain in processing and regulating memories and emotions. When a snarling dog tries to bite you, your fear registers and forms a biochemical association linked to that memory. Which explains why you instinctively avoid an aggressive, snarling dog the next time you encounter one!

Scientists have found that the hippocampus is often smaller in many depressed people, perhaps as a result of stress hormones inhibiting growth in this vital part of the brain. On a basic level, this may be a physical consequence of posttraumatic stress disorder (PTSD)—the brain becomes overwhelmed by fearful, traumatic experiences even as it's impaired in its ability to process them. I'm no doctor, and this is an oversimplification, but my point is this: *what happens outside of us has consequences for what happens inside us.*

Social Factors

The relationship between what happens around us and what happens inside us in response can be tricky to assess. Rarely can clear catalysts or causal relationships be irrefutably determined. Nonetheless, in the past decades many studies have focused on trying to isolate social causes of depression and identifying factors that play a role in triggering it. As I began researching depression and exploring many such well-known studies, one stood out to me. It focused on the link between our circumstances, our support systems, and rate of depression.

In 1978, sociologist George Brown and psychologist Tirril Harris published *Social Origins of Depression: A Study of Psychiatric Disorder in*

Women, a book chronicling the findings of their research over several years. Growing up during and immediately after World War II, Brown noted the way many people directly involved in the war effort suffered from depression. This made sense to him, but he also wondered why others, equally involved on the front lines, moved on without apparent ongoing effects.

His curiosity and academic studies led to his investigation, along with Harris, of women from a similar age range and lifestyle in South London in the mid-seventies. Of the 458 women they interviewed, they found a conclusive relationship between the frequency and accumulation of adverse life events (losses, changes in lifestyle, family adjustments, etc.) and incidents of clinical depression.

The women who experienced a traumatic triggering event but who had not endured many such events in their life prior to the war, became depressed but then returned to their normal disposition relatively quickly. On the other hand, women with a pattern of such losses and traumatic events experienced ongoing, more pervasive depression after the war that was more resistant to treatment. Brown and Harris also noted that women with what they labeled "stabilizing factors," such as supportive relationships with family and close friends, did not experience depression as often as their counterparts who had no such support systems.

The significance of their findings changed the way depression was viewed and treated. External factors, such as the number of traumatic events and adverse circumstances someone experienced, made them more likely to be depressed. The likelihood of depression also increased without emotional support from close relationships. Social catalysts and external circumstances gained attention as major contributing factors to experiencing depression.

A more recent exploration of depression's causes and most effective treatments builds on the findings of Brown and Harris. Investigative journalist Johann Hari interviewed the world's leading experts on depression and concluded its primary causes stem from a variety of different disconnections. Based on the scientific evidence, Hari identified nine disconnections contributing to depression:

- Disconnection from meaningful, purposeful work
- Disconnection from meaningful relationships with other people
- Disconnection from personal values with intrinsic rewards
- Disconnection caused by trauma in childhood
- Disconnection from self-worth and self-respect
- Disconnection from the natural world
- Disconnection from hope for a better future
- Disconnection in the body and brain due to genetics
- Disconnection in the body and brain due to trauma[5]

Notice that the first seven of these are social (external) in nature while only the last two are biological (internal). As Hari points out, when these disconnections repeatedly overlap, a cumulative tide of depression washes over a person. The impact of ongoing stressors poking at the tender wounds of chronic trauma, over a lifetime, naturally results in depression.

There is considerable hope in Hari's findings, though. The fact that most of these disconnections are external means they can also be addressed and remedied externally. In other words, you and I may have more power than we realize to influence and control the factors contributing to depression.

Addressing Depression from the Outside In

I'm biased toward these studies about connections between external and internal factors because they not only resonate with my personal experience of depression, but also with what I find in God's Word. As you'll find in the chapters ahead, the disconnections Hari identified parallel some foundational biblical principles for living a fulfilling life, enjoying the gifts of God's creation, and using our gifts to leave an eternal legacy.

Before you can begin to explore these principles, however, you must be honest—with yourself and with God—about your experiences, your thoughts, your feelings, and your overall health. Identifying the causes of your depression will require some detective work, and that can be frustrating if you're looking in the wrong places or denying your depression in the first place. Some aspects of depression are indeed beyond your control, but I'm convinced many of them are within your power to change and improve.

So what can you do to get started? Here are three steps you can begin to take in this very moment.

ACCEPT THAT OVERCOMING DEPRESSION IS A PROCESS RATHER THAN A QUICK FIX

Depression is complex and reflects each person's DNA, life experiences, physical and mental health, current circumstances, and spiritual belief system. Experts estimate that at least half the cases of serious depression go undiagnosed or unaddressed by those suffering.[6] So don't ignore that feeling you know is there, like the one I first had two decades ago when I knew something was off-kilter in my life.

BE HONEST ABOUT WHAT YOU ARE EXPERIENCING

Pay attention to your emotions, appetite, sleep patterns, and exercise habits. Write down how you're feeling each day, describing as honestly as possible what's going on inside you. Reflect on what you know you enjoy doing and the last time you felt pleasure doing it. Ask a handful of those closest to you what they see in how you relate to them and engage with daily responsibilities. Also note any changes in what or how much you're eating as well as any weight gain or loss. Document how many hours of sleep you get each night and list any disruptions to your sleep patterns. Assess your physical activity—are you active, sedentary, or somewhere between?

Ask God to Reveal to You Where You Are—and Trust He Will Reveal Himself to You There

Ask for the Lord's help as you begin exploring how to overcome depression; it is one of the most important steps you can take. Trust that he is with you in this, no matter how alone you may feel or how detached you are from church, Bible study, prayer, or spiritual habits you used to practice faithfully. You may need to reconsider what you're assuming about who God is and how much he loves you. He has never abandoned you and he never will. God will meet you in your doubt, your fear, your anger, your anxiety, and in the deep, dark cave of your depression.

God met Elijah there and called him out for a divine purpose.

God will meet you in your cave as well.

And if you're willing to trust him, he will lead you out of the darkness.

CHAPTER 3

Removing the Stigma

The problem with the stigma around
mental health is really about the stories
we tell ourselves as a society.
—MATTHEW QUICK

People thought I was okay, but I wasn't.

Even now, I hate to admit I was there, but I was. It was one of the toughest things I had ever gone through—and I wasn't sure how I was going to come out the other side. I can only tell the story now in the hope it will help you. Had I experienced this battle when I was younger, the emotional strain might have kept me silent, but not today.

Simply put, I was not okay. I never seriously contemplated ending it all, but I was looking for some kind of escape. I considered resigning and maybe starting somewhere else. But where? And doing what?

I knew instinctively that what I was feeling had the potential to follow me like the proverbial dark cloud over my head no matter where I went. It wasn't the distance between locations that would make a difference; it was the distance between my head and my heart. This was an issue of internal geography.

Now that I'm on the other side of things, writing about it feels embarrassing. Should I keep this to myself? I still worry that people who see me as a "great leader" will discover how fragile I've been. Even now I wonder what the people of Church of the Highlands will think. The few I've already told seemed quite surprised that I struggled with thoughts of quitting.

But I did.

It's been said that confession is good for the soul but bad for the reputation. I've decided it's a risk worth taking. Maybe sharing my story will help someone who is in a similar place. Perhaps someone who faces overwhelming challenges will find a foothold. Or someone who cannot imagine a way forward will find hope.

Maybe my story will help *you*.

My Darkest Cave

Immediately after the tragic death of George Floyd by police in Minneapolis in May 2020, I knew I wanted to address the horrific brutality and systemic racism spotlighted on our national stage in my sermon that following Sunday. My heart was broken by everything I learned and saw related to Mr. Floyd's tragic death, as well as that of many other Black women and men killed in similar situations. With so many voices weighing in, I felt compelled to share the Bible's message of love, acceptance, forgiveness, justice, and human dignity for all people.

And I knew it wouldn't be easy, nor should it be.

Growing up in the South, I had observed racism on many levels. It always troubled and grieved me, but especially so after I committed my life to Jesus and tried to follow his example. In both his words and actions, he made it clear that every human being has worth and value in the eyes of God.

So my heart was already heavy as I prepared my message for that weekend. My spirit was troubled and my mind overwhelmed by the civil unrest, divisive voices, violence, and rioting. Then that Friday night, someone I had never met posted their observations about me on social media. They noted some of my past "likes" on social media seemed to deny both White privilege and the systemic racism woven into the fabric of our country since its founding on the backs of enslaved Black men and women.

The social media post went viral and sparked an online inferno. Suddenly, I was bombarded with hundreds of comments and e-mails, and even some threats on my safety and that of my family. Some who attended our church considered leaving. Some local government and civic agencies cut ties with our church, our community outreach, and the services we provide. Others denounced our church in sweeping generalizations.

My heart felt squeezed in a vise-grip of competing agendas and politicized extremes. The posts that I had "liked" affected people and their assessment of everything about me in ways I'd never considered or imagined. I hated the devastating impact my social media activity was having on my life's ministry. I had always worked hard to make our church services and events welcoming to all people, and I had been so happy to see Church of the Highlands grow into the largest diverse church in our state. I had always done everything I could to set an example of service to others, for no other reason than the humble, holy example set by my Savior.

We had worked so hard to serve all people, to create an outreach hub called the Dream Center that offered relevant resources to our community, including mentoring, meals, and a free health clinic. We hosted blood drives and home repairs, and partnered with other churches to extend our reach to those in need. When the coronavirus pandemic hit, we offered free COVID-19 testing before any of our local government agencies and hospitals. We made and distributed hundreds if not thousands of masks and helped other ministries with their online services.

But some wanted to discount all the good our church had done, and it killed me. It made me sick to think that anyone believed for a second that I would treat anyone differently because of their race, ethnicity, or the color of their skin. And as the currents of our cancel culture converged into a tsunami, I struggled to hold on.

I thought about quitting and running away to hide, just like Elijah.

I couldn't bear to live with the possibility I had inadvertently unraveled my entire life's ministry. That I had hurt people without even realizing it. That I had not only tarnished our church's reputation but had brought shame to the only One I wanted to glorify and honor.

I was in the darkest cave of my life.

And I could not see a way out.

It's Okay Not to Be Okay

When faced with a traumatic event or crisis, people usually default to fight, flight, or freeze mode. And in the wake of something I never saw coming nor could have begun to imagine, I froze. I went numb at first and felt like I was on autopilot, desperate to wake up from a nightmare. Everything hit me so fast that I couldn't think straight or see a way through to understand the magnitude of what had happened and quench the firestorm on social media. I let other people make decisions for me as I tried to come back to myself and find my voice.

For the first time in my life, I seriously thought about quitting everything I had devoted my life to building. I imagined walking away from it all and just disappearing. I wasn't tempted to take my own life, but I was sorely tempted to kill my calling. It just seemed easier than enduring the layers of pain, confusion, sadness, anger, fear, and, of course, depression. I wasn't sure what recovering from this storm looked like, let alone where to begin. I wondered how I could ever help others again if I couldn't help myself.

I began to consider other careers and imagine myself living outside of any kind of full-time ministry role. I had always felt like my entrepreneurial tendencies might help me find success in the business world. Although I never filled out any applications, I did call a few business friends and drop the hint that I was considering other vocations. I even sort of enjoyed the thought sometimes, like an imaginary friend offering consolation, a strange and desperate source of comfort. And, if I'm honest, it also felt like a way of running from God. Wasn't I giving him everything I had in every corner of my life? And this was what I got for it? A life that seemed to be collapsing around me?

As days dragged on, I sensed my cave becoming darker and darker. I struggled to get my bearings and considered silencing my voice within the walls of my pain, telling no one how I really felt. If I acted normal maybe people wouldn't know how broken I was inside. Maybe I could fake it until I made it.

But denying everything was falling apart would have been the worst possible thing for me to do. Although my life felt incredibly unstable, I found that the first shaky step toward restoration was being willing to say that it was all a mess. It was painful to admit, "I am not okay," but the admission was what finally enabled me to see my situation clearly and deal with it.

Through the support of my family and my mentors, I was able to come out of my cave. My wife, my best friends, and my pastor listened and prayed and shared my struggle. Admitting I was not okay and getting help was a crucial step—but it wasn't easy.

As simple and obvious as it may sound, knowing it's okay to not be okay is a lesson it has taken me most of my life to learn. Some days, I feel like it's the sum of what fifty-seven years of life and thirty-seven years of ministry have taught me. So wherever you are and whatever you're experiencing, I'll say it directly to you: *It's okay to not be okay.*

All of us go through things.

And when we get to those places, God will not abandon us. He never has.

While his presence may or may not be felt when you're in your cave of depression, he is moving and speaking through other people. It's ironic that admitting my struggle was so difficult because I had already written about, taught, and instilled the value of community into the foundation of our church. We're committed to small groups and build them around this very principle: we need each other.

> We need a safe place to be when we're lost in the messy places of life.
> We need others to care and just listen and be with us in the midst of it.
> We need to be transparent and vulnerable when we go through hard things.
> We need to take off the mask and find healing.

It's the only way to come out of the cave.

Help Yourself

Trusting others requires openness and vulnerability—we have to stop holding back and keeping things to ourselves. Sharing what's really going on also means we can't lie to ourselves, remain in denial, or pretend we can magically avoid consequences, both internal and external. We have to stop worrying about what others will think if we're vulnerable and worry more about what could happen to us if we continue to keep everything within us on lockdown.

We've got to refuse to carry the stigma of being honest and transparent, especially when it comes to depression, anxiety, emotional distress, and mental illness.

Looking back, I still can't believe what happened and some of the ways I responded. But now I also feel gratitude that I am on the other side—stronger, better, and with a few scars to show for it. I'm so grateful I didn't hide, which I would have done in my younger years. I'm so glad I didn't act on my thoughts telling me to quit, to move on to something else. To run and hide in my cave of despair.

My life is so much better because I went through that hard time. But in the moment I couldn't imagine my life would ever feel better— because I sure didn't feel like trying to move forward and walk through it.

We must stop ignoring the signals that we're in trouble and telling ourselves that they're a sign of weakness. We need to acknowledge the signals for what they are—an indication that we're struggling and need to ask for help. Even when taking medication to treat depression may be necessary, we still have to get in touch with what we're feeling and what's really going on.

You can't get the help you need and begin coming out of your cave until you admit that's where you are! You have to stare down whatever sense of shame or stigma or weakness you've attached to depression. You have to remember that it's a disease, that the pain and distress you feel can either drive you deeper into hiding or help you identify the cause and address it.

We totally understand when someone gets physically sick.

We don't think any less of a person when they have the flu.

We show kindness, compassion, and consideration when someone breaks a leg.

So we have to regard depression with a similar attitude of caring—both for ourselves and for others.

It's not a sin to be sick, physically or mentally. Our illness is not our identity. So why is it still so hard to see it? And why is it so especially hard to see it when we're in the middle of it?

Perhaps it's because we have a wrong view of what depression and anxiety actually are. No doubt, very real medical and chemical factors are at play when we experience depression, but if we only regard the problem biologically, we may limit our view of causes and cures.

What if there might be more going on in our depression than chemistry?

What if our depression is more than a medical malfunction?

What if our pain is pointing us to something more?

What if what we're feeling reveals something we need, something we're missing, something we're supposed to do?

Dealing with the biological factors is important, but what if it's not enough?

The feelings of depression are real—all too real. But they are not a sign of weakness or craziness. They are indicators of greater concerns. The feelings simply make us aware that there's an issue to attend to and a step to take. If we will respect our feelings and look for the light, we will begin to see that there is a life of freedom, health, and real solutions just ahead.

But we have to move beyond the stigma, the shame, the embarrassment.

We have to be willing to help ourselves.

Compassion and Conviction over Condemnation

When we are in the throes of depression—or know people who are struggling with depression, anxiety, or mental illness—we need to treat ourselves and others the way Jesus treats us—with compassion. Compassion begins by recognizing our human limitations, brokenness, and even sin. We acknowledge that we live in a fallen world and suffer the consequences as a result. And we acknowledge that the selfish sin nature inside of us is in direct competition with God's plan for our lives. The good news of the gospel is that Christ made it possible for us to be healed, forgiven, and restored. But before we can experience those things, we have to acknowledge what's hurting, broken, or wrong.

When you're battling depression, you don't have to prove anything to anyone—least of all, God. He is for you and meets you right where you are. Just as he sent his angel to prepare bread and water to nourish Elijah, God will provide what you need to regain your strength, both physically and emotionally. He wants to give you a new life that's purposeful and fulfilling.

The enemy, however, wants to rob you of your life. If he can't kill you, then he'll settle for making you miserable and ineffective. "The thief comes only to steal and kill and destroy," Jesus said. "I have come that they may have life, and have it to the full" (John 10:10). If you think there's no hope for you or that you're past the point of no return, it's a lie! God can heal and transform that which appears and feels impossible to you and me.

I love how honest the apostle Paul was about his own struggles:

> I've tried everything and nothing helps. I'm at the end of my rope. Is there no one who can do anything for me? Isn't that the real question?
>
> The answer, thank God, is that Jesus Christ can and does. He acted to set things right in this life of contradictions where I want to serve God with all my heart and mind, but am pulled by the influence of sin to do something totally different. (Romans 7:24–25 THE MESSAGE)

Paul's statement nails one of the central questions that weighs on us in the midst of depression: "Is there no one who can do anything for me?" When you're in the midst of hard times and also confronting your own shortcomings and mistakes, the existential realities of life are no longer remote or abstract concepts. Your fears, frailties, and frustrations loom front and center. Your body reminds you that this life is temporary. You despair of ever making a difference in the world.

But there is hope! There is grace and forgiveness and new life. Life has meaning and purpose. On the heels of describing his distress, Paul gives his punch line: "Therefore, there is now no condemnation for those who are in Christ Jesus, because through Christ Jesus the law of the Spirit who gives life has set you free from the law of sin and death" (Romans 8:1–2).

Read that again, slowly: *no condemnation*!

God never condemns. Condemnation means you've got a problem and there's no way out. *Conviction*, on the other hand, says you've got a problem and here's the way out! This is the essence of the gospel. Those of us who are depressed need to understand and embrace this good news. And those of us who know someone who is depressed need to treat them the way Jesus treats us all:

Loving without limit.
Embracing without embarrassing.
Caring compassionately without compromise.
Accepting without approving.

And the same goes for the church.

A Word to the Church

If we really believe the good news is to "heal the heartbroken, announce freedom to all captives, [and] pardon all prisoners" (Isaiah 61:1 THE MESSAGE), those of us in the church had better start talking about what people are really going through and find ways to meet them there. We need to show them the acceptance God shows to us. We must normalize the battles of depression so those who suffer from it will be willing to turn to us for help, comfort, and community.

Satan has done a masterful job of shaming us for how we feel and what we do. But when we don't deal with things in our lives, we fall into a continuous cycle of defeat. To make matters worse, we live in a culture that stigmatizes certain types of brokenness more than others. Sadly, this is true even in the church. Whether we realize it or not, Christians often encourage people to keep hiding because of our subtle, and not so subtle, attitudes and actions toward them. Too often, we heap shame on those who are struggling rather than help them come out of their caves and into the light.

The truth is, our whole world is a fallen, broken mess—not without hope, but messy all the same. We are all broken in different ways. No particular shape of brokenness is worse or better than any other. When I see the remains of houses still standing after a tornado, I don't compare the broken windows of one house to another and think, *Now that one is broken more severely than this other one.* No! Shattered windows, like shattered lives, are all simply in need of repair.

Part of offering real help to those we care about who are suffering from depression requires looking at the "logs" in our own life rather than judging the "specks" we see in the lives of others (Matthew 7:5). We've got to stop stigmatizing brokenness and demonizing fallenness. God helps each of us with whatever shape our fallenness takes.

One of the simplest ways we can begin to extend compassion and acceptance to those struggling with depression is to choose our words with care. However well-meaning we might be, some words do more harm than good, and we need to stop saying them. As a starting point, here's a list of ten things *not* to say.

What *Won't* Help Someone Struggling with Depression

- **Trying harder:** "Come on, now, you can snap out of this! Just try a little harder and I'm sure you'll feel better in no time."
- **Disbelieving:** "You suffer depression? But you're always smiling and seem so positive and upbeat! How can you be depressed?"
- **Over-spiritualizing:** "What does your quiet time look like right now? Maybe you aren't spending enough time reading the Bible. Maybe you should wake up earlier and pray more."
- **Deflecting:** "But you have so much to be thankful for! Just look at all the blessings in your life."
- **Minimizing:** "Well, I'm sure you feel bad, but honestly, it could be so much worse. Did I ever tell you about the time . . . ?"
- **Criticizing:** "If you weren't so hard on yourself, I bet you would feel a lot better. Just try to relax, okay? Don't be such a perfectionist all the time."
- **Comparing:** "I know it's hard for you right now, but have you thought about what it must be like for people suffering bigger losses? Maybe you just need to consider helping others instead of focusing on yourself so much."
- **Dismissing:** "This too shall pass. You'll get over it—I know you will! Just give it a little time."
- **Redirecting:** "Wow, I wish I had your problems. That's nothing compared to what I've been going through. Have I ever told you about . . . ?"
- **Reducing:** "You just need to get out of your head and quit thinking about stuff so much. Lighten up!"

No one wants to hear these responses when they're depressed and anxious. When you say something to someone you care about that implicitly or explicitly conveys, "You don't have to be that way," they will resent you. If you've ever had others say something similar when you're struggling, you know how insensitive such words can be. The speakers might mean well, but their words only leave us feeling more isolated, more alone, more detached.

When we're not okay, we need others who are willing to come alongside us.

We need people who will use their words to shine God's love into the darkness of our cave.

So what *should* you say to someone experiencing depression? How can you help them see a glimmer of God's light while they're still deep in the darkness of their cave? Basically, the rule is to say the same things you want to hear when you are struggling! Here are ten suggestions for how you can use your words to bring light to someone in the darkness of depression.

What *Will* Help Someone Struggling with Depression

- **Committing:** "I'm here to sit with you wherever you are right now. I'll listen and be with you no matter what you're facing."
- **Connecting:** "No matter how alone you feel, I care about you. I want you to know you're not alone."
- **Accepting:** "I care about you and what's going on in your life. Don't hold back. I'm here for you no matter what."
- **Encouraging:** "God loves you right where you are, and I know he loves you too much to let you stay there. Trust him. He is working in you, even if you don't see it."
- **Listening:** "If you can, please tell me what it feels like. I want to listen and understand more of what this is like for you."

- **Being trustworthy:** "I'd like to know what's going on, and I promise to keep it confidential. You can trust me if you need someone to confide in. I'm not here to judge you but to show you I care about you."
- **Supporting:** "We're going to get through this, together."
- **Helping:** "Can I do something practical for you that might be helpful to you right now—clean your house or cook some meals?"
- **Giving hope:** "This is not a dead end. I know God has more for you than this. Let's talk through some options of what might be a helpful next step for you."
- **Offering a new perspective:** "Let's see how we can look at this battle from another angle."

The Bible tells us, "Gracious words are like a honeycomb, sweetness to the soul and health to the body" (Proverbs 16:24 ESV). This is never more evident than when we speak words of life to those in need of deep encouragement.

The Ultimate Win-Win

Let me share one final thought that often encourages me when I'm not doing okay. After Jesus conquered death and rose again, he appeared to people on earth for forty days before his final ascension into heaven. Now, if I were Jesus, I would have wanted to take my "I told you so!" tour and revisit certain Jewish religious leaders ("Ha! Guess what? I won!") and Roman soldiers ("I'm ba-ack! You can't kill me!").

So good thing I wasn't given that opportunity, right? Instead of what you or I might do after rising from the dead, Jesus appeared specifically to three individuals. The first was Mary Magdalene, whom Jesus met just outside the tomb following his resurrection (John 20:11–18). Not only was she a woman, but a fallen woman, many scholars believe. His visit with her broke tradition—and gender barriers—by showing how highly Jesus valued everyone, even those society deemed unimportant or immoral. Their encounter is a reminder that no matter who we are or where we find ourselves in life, God still values us and shows us compassion.

Next, Jesus made it a point to appear to his disciples, and particularly to Thomas, while all of them had locked themselves into an upper room for fear that they, too, might be arrested and suffer as Jesus did. Thomas had previously voiced his doubts about his master's resurrection, but Jesus was willing to do whatever it took for Thomas to realize that he was indeed alive—even if it meant allowing Thomas to put his fingers in the nail wounds on his hands and side (John 20:24–29). The encounter with Thomas reminds us that our doubts and demands don't bother Jesus at all. He reveals himself to us even when we've gone into hiding.

Finally, Jesus connects with his disciple Peter, the only one of the Twelve to flat-out deny knowing him the night and early morning before he was crucified. Jesus had even foretold that Peter would deny knowing him three times, which Peter adamantly denied he would do. But a few hours later, there he was, lying about knowing Jesus before the cock had crowed three times (Luke 22:54–62). And yet, Peter's betrayal didn't prevent Jesus from choosing Peter to be a foundational leader of his church. In a beautiful encounter on the shores of the Sea of Galilee, the Lord forgave Peter and restored him (John 21:15–19). Jesus saw beyond the emotional denials in the midst of the worst night of Peter's life. Jesus' message to Peter is the same message he speaks to us: *Your past is your past and I still love you. I see who you are—who you really are, as my Father created you—and want you to thrive. I want to use you and have you represent me to everyone you encounter.*

Jesus meets you right where you are. He has defeated death and he is more powerful than anything that could ever come against you. His victory is your victory. He invites you to share in his triumph, the ultimate win-win.

It's okay to not be okay.

But don't settle for a lifetime of "not okay."

God is calling you out of your cave.

PART 2

Contributing Causes

CHAPTER 4

Life Imbalance

If we're burning the candle at both ends,
we're not as bright as we think we are.
—RICK WARREN

Please—don't let me die!" I begged.

I looked from the stoic face of one paramedic to the other. Focused on loading my gurney into an ambulance on the side of a busy Australian highway, they seem unfazed by my desperate plea. My heart felt like it was being squeezed tighter and tighter. Breathing felt like taking tiny sips of water while dying of thirst.

"I just want to go home so I can see my family one more time . . . please."

As I closed my eyes, I knew my words were intended for God more than anyone else. I surrendered to unconsciousness as the ambulance raced me to the nearest hospital, almost thirty minutes away. Would I wake up in a hospital more than nine thousand miles away from home? Or open my eyes before God in my eternal home?

Obviously, I lived to tell the story, but at the time I truly believed I might die. In hindsight, the events leading up to that scene intersected to create a perfect storm for a panic attack—and a turning point for restoring balance in my life.

I'd arrived several days earlier, landing in the morning Australian time and rushing through customs and immigration to meet my hosts, who then whisked me away to the venue where I would be speaking and ministering most of the day. Adrenaline and Starbucks got me through, and after a fitful night trying to sleep, I flew to another city on the western coast of Australia to preach at an evening church service. Restful sleep continued to elude me, and the next day, Saturday, we flew to another city where I led more services at another church. By Sunday morning, when I stood before a thousand or more people eager to hear my message, I knew I was pushing my limits. My heart was racing, and I felt jittery from the rocket-fuel coffee I drank constantly.

I knew if I could just get through that service, I would have some time to rest and catch my breath before traveling to yet another location for a weeklong pastor's conference. A local friend, also a pastor, offered to drive me that evening, and I was grateful for the down time. We talked and caught up just as the sun began to set and paint the horizon in bands of gold, pink, and orange. The beautiful vista invited me to slow down and calm myself for the first time since landing.

Then my body jolted like I had never experienced before.

My heart accelerated like an engine in overdrive as adrenaline surged through me. I couldn't catch my breath and my mouth went dry. Then an enormous weight began squeezing my chest tighter and tighter. When my arms began tingling, I assumed I had to be having a heart attack and shouted, "Pull over!"

After my ambulance trip to the nearest hospital, I spent the night with doctors and technicians running various tests on my heart. When my doctor told me I had not had a heart attack but a severe panic attack, I decided to discharge myself. After much deliberation, I chose to honor my commitment to speak at the pastor's conference that week before flying home.

Back in Birmingham, I knew I couldn't ignore or minimize what had happened. So I saw a cardiologist who was a good friend and member of Highlands, confident he would find out exactly what happened so we could make sure it wouldn't happen again. After more tests, he explained how jet lag, excessive caffeine, exhaustion, dehydration, and sleep deprivation worked to stop me in my tracks. "You're not Superman, Chris," he said. "You're human like the rest of us. Your body is trying to tell you to slow down."

Power to Choose

I'm guessing you can relate. Maybe you didn't fly halfway around the world to fall apart like I did, but most of us push ourselves well beyond our limits these days. Our margin, the space between ourselves and our limits, has grown smaller and smaller.

My body kept sending me signals to slow down and recover, to get the rest I needed for healthy functioning. But I just kept ignoring those signals and pushing through. Then, when I finally slowed down, my body really had no choice but to hit red alert in order to get my attention. In extreme physical distress, fear and panic took over.

The source of the problem wasn't my emotions, though.

It was in my lifestyle choices.

The United Nations, in their official statement for World Health Day in 2017, announced we need to talk less about chemical imbalances and more about the imbalances in the way we live.[1] More and more experts—neurologists, psychiatrists, counselors, psychologists, and sociologists—now conclude that depression (and its partner, anxiety) most often results from our lifestyle. In many cases, we're doing it to ourselves. Dr. Stephen Ilardi, a clinical psychologist and depression researcher, expertly sums up the lifestyle problem in his book *The Depression Cure*: "We were never designed for the sedentary, socially isolated, sleep-deprived, poorly nourished, indoor, frenetic pace of modern American life."[2]

Virtually all research on depression concludes that if we have no real social life and daily human connection to others, we're more likely to be depressed. Similarly, if we never get out of the house and away from the computer and experience the beauty of God's creation outdoors, we're more likely to feel depressed. If our diets are unhealthy and our minds are filled with the noise of a broken world, we're more likely to experience depression. One contributing factor in particular stood out to me: if we just exist and never find any real meaning in our lives, depression almost always sets in.

Why is lack of meaning so huge? Because we have psychological needs to not only survive but to find significance in what we do. We crave the fulfillment that comes only from making meaningful contributions to others and to the world around us. We'll come back to this and other factors later, but for now just dwell on the possibility that depression can be a disease of lifestyle.

Again, I'm not denying the role that neurochemicals and hormones play in depression. But I do believe what hundreds if not thousands of experts on depression have concluded in recent years: Lifestyle choices contribute more to depression than we probably realize. If we want to fight and win against depression, we need to make some changes in our habits and routines.

After I discovered that my anxiety attack was caused by my lifestyle and diet, I began making changes, such as getting more sleep and reducing my caffeine intake. While the doctor had also prescribed medication so that "if it ever happens again, take this and you'll be fine," I wanted more permanent solutions. It sounded easier to "take this" than to make significant lifestyle changes, but I wanted to honor the dramatic message I had received Down Under.

In fact, that incident became a landmark event as I began making a balanced lifestyle a priority. I began faithfully keeping a day of Sabbath rest in which I turned off my phone and spent time alone with God as well as enjoyed uninterrupted time with my family and friends. I became more selective about the speaking invitations I accepted and made sure all international travel included at least twenty-four hours for jetlag recovery before my event itinerary started. I exercised more often, focusing on activities I enjoyed, like golf or long walks with Tammy, rather than feeling guilty if I didn't make it to the gym multiple times a week. I stayed hydrated and cut back on sugary carbs. God used my body to send a vitally important message, and now I made sure I not only received it but acted on it.

To be clear, my emphasis on lifestyle choices here is not intended to negate or minimize the suffering of those whose depression is caused by reasons beyond their control. Again, adverse circumstances as well as our genes and biology can contribute to our depression, though they still shouldn't control the outcome of our lives. And there are real neurochemical changes that can happen when you become depressed that make it harder to get out of the cave.

But many of the factors that have been proven to cause depression and anxiety are not in our biology—they are in the choices we make about the way we live. What we often interpret as evidence of depression is symptomatic, not causal, sending us a signal to improve our lifestyle habits. And I share this to give you hope. Because once we understand how our lifestyle habits negatively affect us mentally, emotionally, and physically, we gain a whole new set of potential solutions in addition to the option of medication.

If we can identify what we're doing to negatively impact our mental, emotional, and physical health, we can then make different and healthier choices. And yet I also know that changing habits, patterns, and routines can feel impossible. That's why I'm convinced that no amount of medication or talk therapy alone can eliminate depression in our lives. Only God and his Word have the kind of power required to transform us at the deepest levels.

Motion Sickness

If depression is often lifestyle-based, how can behaving differently make us feel differently? The answer, I'm convinced, is best summed up by the great psychologist Dr. George W. Crane in his classic book *Applied Psychology*: "Remember, motions are the precursors of emotions."[3] Think about that for a moment. You control your motions. If you want to stop reading right now and go grab a snack, you can. If your foot itches, you can scratch it. If you're supposed to meet someone, you can walk to the coffee shop or meeting place. You decide how, when, where, and why to put your body in motion.

Emotions, on the other hand, not so much. We all learned early on that our emotions seem to descend on us, erupt within us, and occur in ways beyond our control. Consider the way you involuntarily withdraw your hand when it gets too close to a flame. Instantly, the message goes from the surface of your fingertips to your brain so you don't even have to think about it. Involuntary action is your body's mechanism to prevent you from experiencing harm.

Similarly, certain events and circumstances trigger emotions for most of us. When someone we love dies, we might feel deep sadness, loss, anger, or grief. When we taste our favorite dessert, we feel pleasure, comfort, and delight. When we're driving and someone cuts us off, we're instantly angry. And on and on it goes. We could catalog many well-known triggers and the emotions they initiate in most of us.

Sometimes, however, we're caught off guard by unexpected feelings that may or may not relate to identifiable triggers. We become enraged by something small and seemingly insignificant. We feel sad and cry for no apparent reason. We well up with love and compassion for someone we don't know. Similarly, we often aren't aware of specific triggers pulling us into the dark cave of depression. But I suspect those triggers are there nonetheless. We have simply disregarded or minimized them.

During my trip in Australia, I deliberately ignored my body's signals for rest, sleep, and recovery time. I had grown accustomed to bulldozing my way through fatigue, exhaustion, and depletion so I could do what I believed I must do. I used caffeine to stimulate my body into action, a temporary fix at best, instead of acknowledging my legitimate need for rest.

My emotions tried to signal me to slow down, stop, and catch my breath. But once again, I ignored the feelings of anxiety, fear, anger, and powerlessness that were telling me to hit pause and take care of myself. Instead, I focused on how I wanted others to experience me at these events—as someone warm, engaged, passionate about my faith, high energy, and strong enough to overcome the physical and mental limitations of most human beings. Jet lag? No problem! I was an experienced traveler who knew how to handle something as trivial as jet lag. I hadn't made any conscious and deliberate decisions about these things—at least, not initially. But the truth is that at some level, I knew exactly what I was doing.

Just like I'll bet you have an idea of the physical and emotional signals you ignore.

Pivoting vs. Paralysis

If motions can be controlled by our choices and emotions tend to follow our motions, then the solution seems simple, right? We should just make better choices. Different motions will lead to different emotions. If you're thinking, *That's easier said than done, Chris*, I agree with you. I'm not saying such changes are easy to implement, but I'm guessing, if you think about it, you can identify areas of your life in which you wish you had healthier habits.

And I believe it's not always as hard as we make it out to be.

In fact, recent studies demonstrate that even baby steps can create a shift in the way you feel. It's not that the new habit itself flips a switch in your emotions, but *moving* to act, rather than allowing difficult feelings to paralyze you, can become a pivot that points you in a new direction emotionally.

Taking action in the midst of depression provides dual benefits. When you make better choices, you feel better. When you feel bad, however, you still have the opportunity to make a choice that could change your mood and move you closer to stepping out of your cave. If you think through actions you could take to move forward just a little when you're depressed, it can keep you from getting stuck there. Basically, you identify an action you can take when you feel an emotion that contributes to your depression: *When I feel (emotion), I can (action).* For example:

> *When I feel sad, I can look for something—or someone—to make me laugh.*
> *When I feel down, I can sing an upbeat song.*
> *When I feel afraid, I can pray and claim one of the many promises of God's Word.*
> *When I feel discouraged financially, I can brainstorm steps to save money.*
> *When I feel incompetent, I can list my past successes.*
> *When I feel insignificant, I can write out new goals.*

You may never feel like you can control your emotions the way you might like, but you can do something to contain them. While we'll explore what this looks like in more detail going forward, for now, consider what it might look like for you to take responsibility for how you feel most days. Don't blame yourself or criticize your inability to feel better immediately. Simply consider how different choices might help you pivot your emotions. Something as simple as getting up twenty minutes earlier to pray and spend time in silence with God might make a huge difference. Eating something healthy for breakfast to fuel your body might make a noticeable difference. Connecting with someone and encouraging them might make a big difference.

When you feel depression dragging you into the depths of the cave, you can surrender and become paralyzed, or you can take action and pivot.

Handwriting on the Wall

Recognizing that you still have choices when you're feeling depressed, anxious, or overwhelmed is essential to leaving your cave. The moment you realize what's going on, you can choose to set yourself in motion. Holocaust survivor, humanitarian, and psychiatrist Victor Frankl believed that even in the most horrific, dire circumstances, we still have the power to choose: "Between the stimulus and the response there is a space, and in that space is your power and your freedom."[4] In other words, we can react in default ways—fight, flight, or freeze modes. Or we can hit pause and claim the power to consider our options and what we need or want to do in that moment.

God often creates such moments of awareness in our lives when he sends a message inviting us to a better way. We see a dramatic example of this during an encounter the prophet Daniel had with the king of Babylon, Belshazzar. Hosting a great banquet for a thousand noblemen, the king used gold goblets stolen from the temple in Jerusalem to serve wine to his guests along with their wives and concubines. In addition to celebrating his lavish lifestyle, the king flagrantly mocked God by using sacred temple artifacts as tableware for his party. Nonetheless, God still sent the king a warning:

> Suddenly the fingers of a human hand appeared and wrote on the plaster of the wall, near the lampstand in the royal palace. The king watched the hand as it wrote. His face turned pale and he was so frightened that his legs became weak and his knees were knocking. (Daniel 5:5–6)

Talk about getting your attention! The king definitely took notice, but he had no way to understand what had been written on the wall, so he called in the wise men.

> The king summoned the enchanters, astrologers and diviners. Then he said to these wise men of Babylon, "Whoever reads this writing and tells me what it means will be clothed in purple and have a gold chain placed around his neck, and he will be made the third highest ruler in the kingdom." (v. 7)

And as it turned out, none of the wise men could tell the king what the writing meant. But God's prophet, Daniel, could translate it. Here is what these words mean:

> *Mene:* God has numbered the days of your reign and brought it to an end.
> *Tekel:* You have been weighed on the scales and found wanting.

Peres: Your kingdom is divided and given to the Medes and
Persians. (vv. 26–28)

The message was a prophetic warning, and one that was swiftly
fulfilled when Belshazzar refused to heed it. That very night, the king
was slain and his kingdom captured by Darius the Mede (v. 30). At
first glance his story may not seem connected to depression, but I wonder if we're often warned just as dramatically about changes we need
to make in order to obey God and steward our health. We may not be
as arrogant, overt, and idolatrous as Belshazzar in our bad habits, but
God still gives us reminders about our ability to make better choices.
What if our symptoms of depression are God's handwriting on the
wall in our lives?

Think of it this way. When someone throws up, it's not the
problem but merely a symptom of something going wrong in the body.
When we experience exhaustion, irritability, lack of interest, sleep-
lessness, and extremes of appetite, we often assume depression is the
culprit causing these problems. But what if these issues aren't caused
by depression but are simply the cumulative impact of life imbalance?

With this possibility in mind, let's consider each of Belshazzar's
three warnings and how they can apply to us.

Warning 1: *Mene*

Mene, which literally means "numbered," reminds us that our days
are numbered. King Belshazzar failed to realize the brevity of life and
wasted his in pursuit of vain pleasures, wealth, and power. When we
realize how short our life is, we understand that we must invest it for
eternity. Anytime we think we have more than we need, we tend to
waste whatever it is. But if it's limited, we have to spend it wisely. "Our
days are numbered" reminds us that our life is created by God, and
we have a limited amount of time to live out our God-given purpose.

I believe we all inherently know that we're here for a reason. We may not know as many details about our purpose as we'd like, or have the perfect conditions for fulfilling it. But once we experience God's calling in a divine direction, we're motivated by more than what feels good in any given moment. God gives us a vision bigger than who we are and what we want, something eternal that glorifies him and advances his kingdom.

But our calling has a competitor.

Busyness ensnares us as the drone of incessant demands buzzes through our minds. We're so distracted by the urgent that we lose perspective and give in to what seems to require our attention and energy in the moment, only to realize later we've missed out on giving ourselves to what we care about most. Other people's agendas for our lives eclipse our own. We want to please them and be a good spouse, parent, sibling, friend, neighbor, coworker, and team member. But what they want and think they need from us is not necessarily our own priority. If we don't take control of our lives, somebody else will.

WARNING 2: *TEKEL*

Tekel literally means "weighed" and reminds us how easily our lives get out of balance. When you look at how you used your time—this week, this day, the last couple of hours—how balanced is it? In other words, if you put your activities on one side of a scale and what matters most to you on the other side, would the scale be balanced or out of balance? How well does the way you spend your time align with what you really care about? If God were to weigh your life right now, would it please him? Or would it be found lacking?

Or, consider it from a relational perspective. If you asked your spouse how balanced your life is right now, what would he or she say? How about your kids? Your closest friends? Our crazy schedules pack in way more than most healthy human beings would ever attempt in a given day. We're juggling home repairs and homework, leading board meetings and Bible studies, chauffeuring kids and elderly parents, all while trying to give 110 percent at work, 120 percent at home, and whatever might be left to church, other ministries, and nonprofits.

To make matters worse, we often spend whatever free time or thin margin we have left on social media, ingesting new updates, opinions, and headlines every sixty seconds. We might give our physical bodies the chance to rest, but not our minds. Who can sustain such an imbalanced way of living?

An overwhelmed schedule produces an underwhelmed soul. Attempting to cram as much as possible into each and every day is what I call a "two-handful" mentality. Because we have two hands, we feel pressured to keep both filled at all times. We assume that if we *can* do something, then we *should* do it. Not true! Scripture says, "Better one handful with tranquility than two handfuls with toil and chasing after the wind" (Ecclesiastes 4:6). Not everything doable is sustainable. Just because we can doesn't mean we should. It's better to know your limits, uphold your boundaries, and create margin in your life.

Warning 3: *Peres*

Peres literally means "divided." Pulled and pushed by the many demands on us, we compartmentalize our lives and thereby fracture our wholeness. We're trying to hold everything together, but we're broken and becoming separated into pieces. If we don't change, our lifestyle will destroy us.

Our misuse of time will always cost us something. Our minds, hearts, and bodies will send us signals. God will send reminders to get our attention.

But it's up to us to read the writing on the wall and to make the changes that restore wholeness.

Take Inventory

One of the most powerful tools I've discovered for maintaining balance in my life is a weekly inventory. If you've never done one, you might be surprised how revealing an inventory can be.

I keep my inventory simple and use it to discern what's essential. As I look back over my week, I ask myself questions such as these:

> What patterns or themes do I see?
> Which activities are affecting my emotions positively? And
>   negatively?
> How can I change or redirect those activities that cost too much
>   energy, time, and focus?

Along with the psalmist, I pray, "LORD, remind me how brief my time on earth will be. Remind me that my days are numbered—how fleeting my life is. You have made my life no longer than the width of my hand. My entire lifetime is just a moment to you; at best, each of us is but a breath" (Psalm 39:4–5 NLT).

I evaluate my life in twelve areas, assessing how I did in each area over the past week by asking the questions I listed above. Then I write a sentence expressing what I can change to create more balance in that area in the coming week. Here is my "divine dozen."

Faith	Social
Marriage	Attitude
Family	Finances
Work	Creativity
Computer	Physical
Ministry	Travel

You may have different categories, but you get the idea. We all have areas that tend to dominate the others and put our lives out of balance. We all have time wasters that can be eliminated, whether it's another work meeting that really doesn't require our presence or Internet surfing before bedtime. The very act of making new decisions for the coming week can be empowering and help you feel good as it gets started.

Stop trying to do everything and consider what God has called you to do. Stop saying yes to everything and look for ways to strengthen boundaries around your priorities. If it isn't a clear yes, it's likely a clear no. It might mean allowing margin between appointments or eliminating commitments that drain too much out of you for what they accomplish. Focus on making your greatest contribution to the people and priorities you cherish most. Use your weekly inventory to help you discern what to eliminate and what to implement.

How can you figure out what matters most to you? Here's a filter I've found helpful. Ask yourself, "Will this matter a hundred years from now?" You'll discover there are few things that really matter. In the grand scheme of things, I believe only three areas are worthy of all we can give: God, others, and eternity.

God, Others, and Eternity

Many of us say that God comes first in our lives, but the way we spend our time, money, and affections point to other priorities. Jesus shared the story of a very successful person who focused on wealth instead of God, tearing down his barns to build bigger ones to store the overflowing abundance of his possessions. In the end, the man lost what was most important. "God said to him, 'You fool! This very night your life will be demanded from you. Then who will get what you have prepared for yourself?' This is how it will be with whoever stores up things for themselves but is not rich toward God" (Luke 12:20–21).

Investing in relationships is always important—not every relationship, but the ones that are integral to who God has called us to be and where he has placed us. We need to invest ourselves as much as possible in relationships with those who enhance, nourish, encourage, and sustain our lives. Conversely, we need to distance ourselves as much as possible from those who rob us of life. We need relationships in which we can be real with others who share our faith so we can shoulder one another's burdens and celebrate one another's joys.

Investing in an eternal legacy is also worthy of all we can give. Jesus told a parable that really puts this in perspective. A man found a treasure in a field and sold everything he had to buy that field: "The kingdom of heaven is like treasure hidden in a field. When a man found it, he hid it again, and then in his joy went and sold all he had and bought that field" (Matthew 13:44).

Eternal treasures are the moments that bring us closer to God and that illuminate the lives of others with God's goodness, peace, provision, and power. We invest in an eternal legacy when we do what we're made to do so that God's kingdom grows and overcomes the darkness in this world.

Elijah did what God asked him to do, but his life still seems to have become imbalanced. After Jezebel's threat, Elijah ran for his life and kept going for thirty days with no break in the action. As we will soon explore, God first sent an angel to provide food and water for Elijah and to encourage him to sleep. Before God met him in his cave, the Lord made sure Elijah's basic needs—for nourishment, hydration, and rest—were met.

Maybe you haven't allowed yourself to become so rundown, at least not yet, but your life is tilting toward depletion. You may be only considering your short-term wants instead of your long-term needs. Knowing that your life is short, knowing that you have a finite amount of time and resources, what does an inventory of your life reveal? What areas are out of balance? How do they contribute to your experience of depression and anxiety?

For too long, *how* you live may have determined *where* you live—in a dark cave. But you have the ability to make different choices. Take a step. Just one step.

The light is right in front of you.

CHAPTER 5

Scrolling Away My Peace

Comparison is the thief of joy.
—THEODORE ROOSEVELT

It used to control me.

When I say *control me*, I mean it determined how I felt, thought, and sometimes acted. Comments and comparisons. Likes and follows. Tweets and reposts. That's what social media was for me. Who's saying what and who's doing what? Whom should I be following? Who's following me? Should I post this pic or tweet that quote?

Something about social media always left me feeling uncomfortable. But I did it because it was the new tool everyone was using to communicate, to expand the church, and to connect with the new generation. When I first got on social media platforms, I saw it as a fun way to keep up with friends, families, and other pastors and churches. I loved sharing posts about my life, my adorable grandkids, special events, and exciting vacations.

I also saw how social media kept our church family informed about all that was going on. It was perfect for sharing real-time prayer requests and celebrating moments and milestones affecting us all. Our church website could livestream services, archive sermons, link to small groups, and list opportunities for members and visitors alike. Online, we could connect with all our Highlands campuses and the churches and ministries we support around the world.

Before long, though, virtual existence began to take a toll. I sometimes spent hours drafting one paragraph for a post, trying to come up with just the right words to avoid potential criticism or misunderstanding. I knew I couldn't please everyone all the time, especially when it comes to matters of faith. Jesus even told his followers, "If the world hates you, keep in mind that it hated me first" (John 15:18). Still, I was often surprised by how critical our culture has become as evidenced online. Over time, I saw more and more comments from self-proclaimed Bible experts claiming something I said contradicted Scripture based on a sound bite or sermon clip they pulled completely out of context.

It was maddening.

Then there were the posts dealing with politics, real-time news, and cultural trends. Every time a big story broke (and aren't they all "big" stories online?), I felt pressured to say something, to offer an opinion whether or not I had one. I quickly realized that commenting on and responding to every online news update could consume every waking hour.

And there were the relational posts, comments, and connections. With our adult children starting families of their own, the number of birthdays to remember has almost tripled. Then there's extended family—aunts and uncles, cousins, and lifelong friends. Do I need to send the same message to every person so no one gets their feelings hurt? Will they think I love them less if I don't like the post they sent me?

I found myself constantly checking for how many likes, comments, and new followers appeared since the last time I'd checked, usually within the previous hour. I quickly scrolled down to see if anyone used my post to promote their own message or to make an ugly comment. I didn't want my posts to be mishandled or distorted by anyone, especially people I had never met.

Inevitably, I began comparing the success of some pastors and the growth of their churches to my own. I couldn't help looking at the work they were doing. It was tough to watch sermon clips with preaching that seemed way better than what I had preached most recently. Rather than inspire me, pastor jokes (you think "dad jokes" are bad!) and funny posts only left me feeling inadequate and wishing I could be that funny and creative.

Please know that I'm not one to envy what others have. I'm very content with what God has given me and thoroughly enjoy my assignment in life. I'm blessed in so many ways I never imagined and humbled to see how the Lord uses me and our church to impact so many people's lives for his kingdom.

But I still noticed other churches and pastors. And it was hard not to compare and feel less-than when we enjoyed a regular Sunday service while the pastor of a church I followed on Instagram baptized thousands—or at least it felt that way—of people! I rejoiced for the kingdom and was happy for the other church—after all, we're on the same team, right? So why did it still not feel so good in my soul?

What did I do? I let the pressure to be more and do better increase within me until its weight grew heavier. Frequently feeling just average, just competent, a C+ in comparison with my ministry peers, I tried harder but never seemed to gain any ground. There were just too many categories to conquer.

I had read something that really resonated with me, about how pastors today are expected to be business savvy, tweet-quotable, and always brimming with positive, upbeat energy as evidence of their faith. We're required to be fully accessible yet deeply spiritual, able to dive from the surface of current events to the depths of eternity in a nanosecond. Not too young and inexperienced and not too old and out of touch. While I knew it wasn't a realistic expectation, I felt immense pressure to be "just right," the pastor Goldilocks would choose when church shopping. And if I only got three out of five stars for this week's sermon, I'd think about how to do better next week.

Comparison culture was eating me alive. With each click, I experienced a reminder of who I would never be, what I seemingly couldn't get right, and where I might never go. Comparing my real life to online highlight reels of others, I felt miserable. Instead of continuing to try harder or, better yet, limiting my time online, I eventually crawled toward my cave, depressed by my deficits.

When No Better Means Worse

Crushed by comparison, I could understand why Elijah ran away and hid in a cave. Because nothing he could do would please his most powerful critics—King Ahab and Queen Jezebel. After the vindictive death threat from Jezebel, Elijah isolated himself: "[He] went a day's journey into the wilderness. He came to a broom bush, sat down under it and prayed that he might die. 'I have had enough, LORD,' he said. 'Take my life; I am no better than my ancestors'" (1 Kings 19:4).

Pretty extreme, right? Why would Elijah conclude he was no better than his ancestors? And what does that have to do with asking God to take his life? I suspect Elijah may have gotten caught up in a culture of comparison just as we do today. If he wasn't any better than his ancestors, then he had failed, which he considered worse. The basis of comparison differs, but the depressing results are clearly the same.

Elijah had his own calling, to be God's prophet and warn the people of Israel to repent from their rebellion against God. Obeying the assignments he received from the Lord, Elijah celebrated amazing victories, especially that epic sacrifice showdown with the 450 priests of Baal. I'm guessing Elijah felt strong in his faith at that moment, perhaps even stronger in his obedience and faithfulness than previous generations of God's people.

After facilitating a spectacular triumph proving the existence and power of the true and only living God, Elijah may have felt like a faith superstar—which ultimately he was—but not for long. Following Jezebel's threat, he was on the run from heads of state who despised him and wanted revenge for the humiliation they had suffered by his display of God's power. Knowing the character and tenacity of Ahab and Jezebel, Elijah may have assumed his death was inevitable. He was weary and depleted, and his enemies were enraged and fully resourced. The faith that had long fueled his life as God's prophet suddenly evaporated in his desert despair.

As a result, Elijah concluded he was just like every other Israelite.

A bandwagon believer. Fickle in his faith.

No better than any of his ancestors whom God had rescued out of bondage in Egypt only to worship a golden calf a short while later. Trusting God for the impossible one day but running in fear when the stakes got personal.

Elijah got caught in the comparison trap, which only made him more depressed.

It happens when we care too much what others are doing.

It happens when we care too much what others are thinking.

It happens when our self-worth hinges on winning a cultural competition—a rigged race that leaves us running in place on a treadmill to nowhere.

The only way to get off this treadmill is to see ourselves the way

God sees us. And we've got to see others the way God sees them too. We must learn to value ourselves and others for who we are: children of God created in his holy image. This lesson pivots on showing grace to ourselves and those around us when we start slipping into comparison and competition instead of cooperation and collaboration. Showing grace doesn't mean we just accept our weaknesses and shortcomings and resign ourselves to remaining in a rut. Instead, grace accepts us where we are, but it also redirects us toward God.

We don't have to be like anyone else or better than anyone else to be accepted by our Abba Father. He only wants us to be all that he created us to be. But seeing ourselves as he does takes practice, and it may feel uncomfortable and unfamiliar at first.

People tell me all the time, "If I could just have the kind of faith that so-and-so has, then I know I could trust God with my life." Or sometimes they're an even harsher critic of themselves: "I'm not a good Christian, Chris. Some days I try harder than others, but I keep struggling with the same old hang-ups. I'll always be a mess."

But that's not what God says. God says that you are "the head and not the tail, and you shall only go up and not down" (Deuteronomy 28:13 ESV). Too often, we assess ourselves in the moment while God sees us from his omniscient, eternal perspective. Just as a parent sees who their child really is beyond the foolish mistakes they make, our heavenly Father doesn't see us as we are, but as we could be. He sees our potential.

Slipping into the Comparison Trap

We all know we're on a slippery slope when we start comparing ourselves to other people. The Bible says over and over, don't do it! Still, we slide into comparison like an old pair of shoes. Comparison is a temptation because we have the ability to choose.

Adam and Eve could eat the fruit of any tree in the garden of Eden except one, but you know which one proved irresistible, right? Tempting them to disobey God, the serpent lured them with, you guessed it, comparison: "God knows that when you eat from it your eyes will be opened, and you will be like God, knowing good and evil" (Genesis 3:5). The enemy held out the illusion of something better, which proved to have devastating consequences when the first man and woman tasted its bitter truth. Adam and Eve bought into the lie that they could be equal with God. They believed this deception rather than accept their unique place and value as God's creation, a comparison trap that still ensnares us today.

While we will never be equals with God, we remain equals with all other human beings! No better, no worse. Everybody is unique and has a distinct role in the epic story God authors with us. There is only one person on the planet you can be, and that is you.

When we try to imitate other people to gain acceptance or prop up our self-worth, we will always fail. We can't be them any more than they can be us. However, rather than accept and celebrate our specialness, we focus on our failure to be someone else—or who we perceive them to be—which only leaves us feeling depressed. We feel hopeless to make a change or be different because we can't be some other person.

But God wants you to be you, because he made you that way.

When we compare ourselves to other people—whether our ancestors, our nemesis at work, or the person we admire so much on Instagram—we get depressed. And comparison traps always end up reinforcing the same conclusion: we will never be good enough, smart enough, wealthy enough, attractive enough, powerful enough, or special enough. In my experience, every comparison trap follows a similar, four-part pattern.

1. WE COMPARE OUR WEAKNESSES TO OTHER PEOPLE'S STRENGTHS.

We forget that those people might also have areas of weakness where we might be strong. We assume the worst about ourselves while taking the strength and talent of others at face value.

2. WE FOCUS ON OUR DEFICITS RATHER THAN OUR VALUE.

Comparing the partial view we have of someone else with the comprehensive view we have of ourselves will always lead us to be critical of ourselves. Our internal critic is usually focused on standards that are unattainable and unrealistic. We use our self-criticism and condemnation to motivate us and wonder why our results aren't the same as the results we perceive others achieving. Basically, we keep "shoulding" ourselves: "I should be more like that person. I should accomplish more. I should make better choices. I should stop those bad habits. I should act better. I should have a stronger faith." But shoulding only reinforces our feelings of inadequacy and failure.

3. WE FALL INTO THE THOUGHT TRAP OF SELF-LABELING.

We cling to the belief that what we do—or have done—is who we are. Combined with self-criticism, we label ourselves based on our mistakes, struggles, and weaknesses. "I'm a quitter," "I can't follow through on anything," or, "I'm such a dummy—I can't do anything right." Instead of "I made a mistake," we conclude, "I'm a total failure."

When we self-label, we take the words that describe our behavior and make them our identity: alcoholic, addict, liar, cheater, adulterer, hypocrite. Name-calling and nagging doesn't work when used on others, yet we struggle to stop name-calling and nagging ourselves.

We label ourselves with disparaging titles that only reflect part of our story instead of remembering our value and looking at the big picture.

4. WE ASSUME OTHER PEOPLE HAVE BETTER LIVES THAN OURS.

Envy is the resentment or lack of contentment we feel when someone else has something—an opportunity, a possession, a quality—we want but don't have. Left unchecked, envy becomes laser-focused on undermining everything good in our lives by comparing it with what we lack. Envy has metastasized in our culture as affluenza, the disease of thinking more is always better: more money, more stuff, more luxury, more celebrity, more fame, more power. Envy contributes to depression like nicotine contributes to cancer, an indefinite deficit consuming our lives.

Screen with Envy

Why is envy so powerful in its toxic ability to poison our lives? When we succumb to envy, we see only the best in others' lives and the worst in our own. Envy thrives on comparison. Others' lives seem always *more* than our own. More exciting. More fun. More fulfilling. More enjoyable.

But it's a self-made illusion. The *more* we see in others' lives isn't real, only a comparative illusion. Envy is like watching a movie or TV show and wondering why our lives seem so mundane. Most of the time, we don't see characters doing laundry, getting the oil changed in their cars, arguing with their kids about bedtime, balancing their checkbooks, taking out the trash, or clipping their nails. Instead, we see the actors wearing beautiful costumes and doing exciting things in perfectly curated sets.

Envy makes contentment impossible. By its very nature, envy always compares and guarantees dissatisfaction. God's Word says, "A heart at peace gives life to the body, but envy rots the bones" (Proverbs 14:30). Like an intersection of two highways that lead in completely different directions, gratitude and envy will leave you either appreciating all the blessings in your life or chasing after whatever you believe will satisfy that hole you're trying to fill inside. "If you look at what you have in life, you'll always have more," Oprah Winfrey has frequently been quoted as saying. "If you look at what you don't have in life, you'll never have enough."

Why can't we be happy where we are, with who we are, and with what we have? Why do we always compare ourselves to others? In other words, what makes envy tick?

For one thing, we have the wrong perspective. Comparison would have us believe that what we have is not good enough and what others have is better. This mentality has existed forever, but social media has fueled it in an extraordinary way. At first, Facebook helped us keep up with people we love, but now it just makes us jealous of everyone! Seriously, just think about the times when seeing something online has triggered envy:

- When you see someone's "Look at my new _____" post
- When others' vacation pics and videos pop up
- When everyone else seems to enjoy weekly family meals and gatherings
- When you notice someone's relationship status has changed to "engaged"
- When a promotion gets celebrated
- When a new car, boat, ATV, or other big purchase gets posted
- When someone's house looks like a photo shoot from a design site

- When cute clothes and new outfits look perfect
- When you notice someone's weight loss, new haircut, or toned biceps

The list could go on and on! Right in front of us, twenty-four seven, we can see virtually everything that we are not or that we don't have. Every vacation we didn't get to take or the spring break trip we did take but it rained the whole time. Every relationship that's stalled, failed, or hurt us. Every family member who has disappointed, annoyed, frustrated, or wounded us. Every success we haven't achieved. Every promotion that passed us by, every job we didn't get, every award we didn't receive. Every pound we gained and every fitness goal we failed to reach.

I'm not against social media (well, maybe I am), but I have to be honest about what I see, which is that it often steals value from our lives. After spending time on social media, our levels of contentment and self-esteem inevitably take a nosedive. Anxiety and stress increase. In an unlimited environment of comparison, we don't measure up. *And we never will.*

When envy taints our attitude and outlook, we develop unrealistic (often impossible) expectations. We think what we don't have would make us happy. We chase it, get it, post a selfie with it, and then wonder why more people online don't seem to notice or care. This self-defeating cycle guarantees that we will be driven by a seductive message: we are unhappy, but happiness is only one step away.

But here's the problem: envy makes happiness a conditional and moving target.

I'm always intrigued when celebrities and people who have incredible success reveal their struggles to be happy. Actor and funny man Jim Carrey said, "I think everybody should get rich and famous and do everything they ever dreamed of so they can see that it's not the answer."[1] He makes a great point because social media taunts us with the possibility of going viral and finding overnight fame, wealth, and recognition. But even if it happens, enough is never enough.

Envy leaves us in a vicious cycle: we compare, feel we don't measure up, get what we think will make us happy, feel disappointed, compare again, and keep the cycle going.

Enough wasn't enough.

It never is.

Let It Go

When envy becomes our default, we focus on the wrong person. We grow so focused on others that we miss out on our own lives. This cultural discontent is known as FOMO—Fear of Missing Out. I doubt you need it defined because you've probably experienced it just like I have. It's that underlying sense that we're losing something we don't even know about. Others are doing things, knowing things, discussing things, possessing things, and posting things that we want to be part of but aren't.

This low-grade anxiety keeps us glued to our phones. *Better check my e-mail—who just texted?*—and we scroll through the latest to see what's going on. We are so connected to people in cyberspace that we are rarely able to be fully where we are and present to those we are with. Instead, our phones are in front of us. We're taking selfies to post to show others where we are and what we're doing—because we're not engaged enough to know ourselves.

How much time do you spend looking at your phone? If you're like the average American, it adds up to a total of about forty-nine days out of the year.[2] That's almost two months of your life each year, staring at a screen. Feeling worse and worse. Experts agree that we've never been so connected and yet so lonely at the same time.[3] Even social media platform creators and contributors are recognizing the monster unleashed by the methods they've monetized. The tagline for the Netflix documentary *The Social Dilemma* is, "The technology that connects us also controls us, manipulates us, polarizes us, distracts us, monetizes us, divides us."[4] Stanford psychiatrist Anna Lembke put it bluntly when she said, "Social media is a drug."[5]

Our addiction to social media feeds on our primal instincts, giving us raw coverage of the latest disaster, impending crisis, or personal scandal. A journalist writing for the *Wall Street Journal* called this "doomscrolling," that unrelenting need to keep reading, scrolling, and checking again and again, no matter how bad it makes us feel.[6]

In my own battle to overcome depression, I decided it was time for me to quit social media. I got to the point where I really didn't see any benefit, only negative emotions keeping me on edge, anxious, afraid, angry, and agitated. For our church and ministries, I'm fortunate to have a team who can manage those platforms for me. The result has been a level of peace I haven't known in many years.

I'm not telling you that you must abstain from social media to be freed from depression. But I am telling you, based on my experience and countless books and articles I have read, that your social media may need to be regulated, reduced, and reconsidered. Because social media is probably the number one pipeline for perpetuating comparison and envy in your life right now.

Elijah never had to worry about seeing what other prophets were saying online.

He didn't have to read snarky comments from Jezebel's fans.

He wasn't worried about looking inferior because of what the priests of Baal were wearing.

But Elijah still compared himself to his ancestors—and felt like he wanted to die.

If you want to come out of your cave, you have to stop comparing.

Because God made you incomparable.

CHAPTER 6

Chewing the Cud

Ninety-five percent of your emotions . . . are
determined by the way you talk to yourself.
—BRIAN TRACY

For me, it's usually Sunday night.

That's when I do the autopsy of everything that happened at church that day. I dissect my message, picking apart every sentence. I review each service, comparing attendance, assessing the music, analyzing everything from the announcements to the benediction. Sunday night is also when my emotions are coming down from a two-day high, because Sundays actually start on Saturday for me. That's when I start gearing up my mind, heart, and spirit to preach.

People often tell me, "You make it look so easy." And that's just it. It *looks* easy. A good sermon doesn't show its seams. I'm like a duck on a pond—gliding gracefully on top but paddling furiously beneath the water. God has given me a grace for what I do, and I am thankful. But there is still that "crash" moment after it's all over, when my body and soul let go.

It's in those moments, usually on Sunday nights, when I'm most vulnerable mentally and emotionally. If the enemy is going to tempt me, it's usually during those hours at the end of a ministry-packed weekend.

My wife, Tammy, knows all about it. I've shared this struggle with her and asked her to stay close during Sunday nights and similar times—and she does. With her help, and the help of the Holy Spirit, of course, I rarely let those moments push me toward trouble or pull me into my dark cave.

Recognize Your Rumination Rut

Psychologists refer to what happens in my Sunday night autopsy routine as "rumination." Clinical psychologist and depression expert Stephen Ilardi explains, "Rumination appears to be an instinctive human response when something goes wrong. It's as if we're hardwired to replay our recent trials and tribulations over and over again in the mind's eye—to mull things over for a while before we're ready to move on."[1]

The word *ruminate* means to ponder something deeply and thoroughly. The same word is used to describe how a cow chews the cud, the back-and-forth process of chewing grass, swallowing it, regurgitating it, chewing some more, swallowing it again, on and on. Gross, perhaps, but it graphically depicts how we fixate on certain thoughts and events.

When we ruminate, we recall events, conversations, situations and go over all the details as thoroughly as possible in our minds. We compare our analysis to our expectations, ideals, and perceptions, usually critiquing our performance or contribution. As many experts, including Dr. Ilardi, point out, such painstaking examination can result in greater self-awareness, better preparation for future situations, and more active participation. People often call this *processing*. But in our culture of comparison, rumination can also paint us into a torturous corner of destructive perfectionism. When that happens, our thinking gets nastier with each round of the chew-swallow-regurgitate cycle.

Seasoned with regret, rumination focuses our attention on the symptoms of our distress rather than solutions to our distress. We overthink or obsess about situations and relationships, looking for insight that will give us more control or help us achieve desired outcomes. But these cycles of negative self-talk often create problems where there are none and make legitimate issues worse. This only leaves us more vulnerable, especially to the enemy who loves to seize any opportunity to distort our internal narrative even more.

Research has shown that habitual rumination results in many negative consequences, including depression, anxiety, and posttraumatic stress disorder (PTSD).[2] Addiction is also prevalent as ruminators try to quiet the internal analysis and ease the pain of their perceptions of imperfection. My Sunday night go-to was mindless TV viewing—sports, old movies, anything to divert my attention from the negative voices clamoring in my head.

What's your rumination trap? What happens at work that you replay in your mind again and again? Which conversations get transcribed and dissected as you try to parse each nuance and figure out how to read between the lines? When do you usually slip into rumination?

Recognizing your rumination rut is often the first step out of it.

Three Consequences of Rumination

While we may ruminate about different things than generations past, the problem is far from recent. In fact, I believe one of the reasons Elijah sank into depression stemmed from his rumination. After winning the sacrifice showdown with the 450 prophets of Baal, the prophet seemed to question everything—his identity, his purpose,

God's ability to protect him, and his future. On the run from royal vengeance, Elijah isolated himself and got into his own head.

We don't know the exact thoughts that played over and over again when the needle got stuck on the record of Elijah's mind. But we do know rumination results in three consequences that contribute to depression. Rumination allows our feelings to define our lives and dictate our actions, makes us harder on ourselves than we should be, and causes us to exaggerate the negative. Let's unpack each one of these.

1. RUMINATION ALLOWS OUR FEELINGS TO DEFINE OUR LIVES AND DICTATE OUR ACTIONS.

What did Elijah do when Jezebel threatened his life? He felt afraid and then he fled (1 Kings 19:3). He was overwhelmed by fear and acted accordingly. That's not always a bad thing, but it can be when it blinds us to reality. Elijah kept running until he came to a broom tree, sat under it, and prayed that he might die. It's not hard to imagine the thoughts that possibly echoed in his mind.

Why would God allow Jezebel to come after me when I did everything he asked me to do?

Why did the king and queen not repent and return to God after seeing his power in contrast with the impotence of Baal? What could I have done differently to produce a different, better outcome?

I'm trying to be God's servant and doing the best I can. But nobody else is paying attention or doing their part—I can't do this alone!

If God's people don't heed the warnings I've given them, then I can't help them. I've had enough. I'm fed up with everyone hating me for telling them the truth!

Nothing makes any difference. I'm through. I'm giving up. Let me die, Lord.

These types of ruminations quickly turn uncertainty into emotion, often retrofitting the facts to our feelings. We question and wonder and ponder and consider other outcomes. We think of what we might have done differently or the part others played. We can't see what God could possibly be doing and allow doubt to dent our faith. Without realizing it, we shift our focus from external reality to internal rumination, which in turn stirs up a storm of emotion within us.

Elijah *felt* like a failure even though he wasn't. He accepted his feelings as facts: *I feel like a failure so I must be one.* Such false conclusions result from emotional reasoning, which is dangerous on many levels. Emotional reasoning covers our senses with filters that reinforce the feeling-based conclusions we've drawn. It lets our heart lead without any balancing input from the rest of us.

The feelings that result from rumination rarely reflect factual reality. But so often we allow our feelings to control us—to influence and determine the choices we make and the actions we take, the habits we make or the ones we break. We make decisions based on our feelings, and the false narratives we create out of them, without recognizing their unreliability, inconsistency, and inaccuracy. The more we ruminate, the bigger and more errant those self-told stories become. We lose perspective on what's true.

Instead of allowing our emotions to lead, we have to consider what's true—both factually and spiritually—and make healthy, reality-based, God-honoring decisions. We choose, act, and allow our feelings to change like weather patterns: one hour sunny, the next cloudy, stormy, or clear.

Many contemporary psychologists say a key to mental health is getting your feelings out in the open. However, recognizing your emotions, accepting them, and deciding how, when, or if to express them will only take us so far. Without the anchor of eternal truth, our feelings still tend to rise and fall with our circumstances. But God's truth sets us free.

Many people are trapped in depression because they're living by their feelings instead of by the promises of God. They feel overwhelmed and struggle to find a bedrock foundation for their lives. Because they feel hopeless about their circumstances, they consider it a fact that their problems are impossible to solve.

What they feel is real—but not necessarily *true*.

2. RUMINATION MAKES US HARDER ON OURSELVES THAN WE SHOULD BE.

Rumination is like viewing ourselves in a funhouse mirror; we see only distorted images of ourselves. Instead of seeing ourselves the way God sees us, we see the labels of our past, of who others say we are, of our worst moments and biggest failures.

Elijah accepted way too much of the responsibility for something that was really not his fault: "I have been very zealous for the LORD God Almighty. The Israelites have rejected your covenant, torn down your altars, and put your prophets to death with the sword" (1 Kings 19:10). If you'll indulge my paraphrase, he basically said, "I have worked my tail off for three years, and the Israelites are not any closer to repentance than before! I have *really* tried here. I've been zealous and obedient and unrelenting in my warnings, Lord, but it hasn't been enough. Nothing I do works!"

In his depression, Elijah blamed himself for failing to change the hearts of an entire nation. He took it personally. Many of us do the same thing—we assume responsibility for things God never intended us to bear. I struggle with this trap all the time with the church I lead, people I counsel, and my children. When something doesn't work out the right way, or in what I consider the right way, then I assume I've failed. Rumination kicks in: *Could this be my fault? Where did this go off the rails? Why did this happen? What could I have done differently?*

There's nothing wrong with asking questions such as these, but it's the obsessive speculation of rumination that fuels depression. People don't always (or usually) respond the way you want them to respond. You assume, expect, and second-guess—but what happens? You feel blindsided; instead of acknowledging the responsibility others have for their own choices, you try to shoulder that responsibility yourself.

Here's the truth, though: *God has given each of us a free will.*

We are each responsible for our choices. Yes, we have responsibilities to love, support, serve, and encourage others. But we cannot take responsibility for the choices of others.

I often carry a burden for someone else and assign responsibility for it to myself alone. It happens almost by default. I don't realize it's happening until I start feeling depressed and powerless to do what I believe should be done—only to be reminded that it's not my responsibility in the first place!

We can influence people, but we can never control them.

Like Elijah, we often ruminate ourselves into self-blame.

Until God clears our vision with what's true.

3. RUMINATION CAUSES US TO EXAGGERATE THE NEGATIVE.

Rumination contributes to our depression when it amplifies criticism and negativity. Elijah's response to his situation implied, "I'm the only obedient, God-fearing person left, and what difference does it make? Now they're trying to kill me too." But was this true?

The fact is that the world was not against him. It was just one vindictive woman named Jezebel, who had taken the defeat of Baal personally, just as Elijah had taken the people's rebellion personally. Jezebel's threat was scary because Elijah allowed her to get in his head. Maybe I'm mistaken, but if Jezebel really intended to kill him, she wouldn't have sent a messenger—she would have sent a hit man!

Regardless of Jezebel's threat to kill him, she knew that her intimidation would take root in the prophet's imagination. She didn't need to follow through when his fears immobilized him and sent him running away.

The enemy does the same with us. Instead of derailing our lives directly, he turns our own thoughts against us—accusing us, speaking fear and insecurity to our hearts, and paralyzing us from pursuing God's best. What we imagine and worry about happening is often far more powerful and enduring than reality. We become so afraid of the loud, angry barking that we fail to realize that its source is a tiny poodle with no teeth hiding behind the gate. We forget to "take captive every thought to make it obedient to Christ" (2 Corinthians 10:5).

If Elijah hadn't let rumination get the best of him, he might have handled this situation differently. Even if Jezebel did intend to kill him, Elijah lost perspective and forgot what he knew to be true: "The LORD is with me; I will not be afraid. What can mere mortals do to me?" (Psalm 118:6). When Jezebel had made threats against God's prophets before, they were protected by the prophet Obadiah: "Haven't you heard, my lord, what I did while Jezebel was killing the prophets of the LORD? I hid a hundred of the LORD's prophets in two caves, fifty in each, and supplied them with food and water" (1 Kings 18:13).

Jezebel knew she didn't have to kill Elijah to get him to stop opposing her. She simply had to induce fear and let his own emotions do the rest. And did they ever!

Elijah took off and ran to the desert and didn't stop until he could hide in a cave. Jezebel silenced the troublesome prophet without having to spill a drop of his blood. She was smart enough to know that his own cave of despair would claim his life more effectively than any torture she could devise. In record time, Elijah went from mighty man of God (1 Kings 18) to scared caveman (1 Kings 19).

Just as we all do sometimes.

The more Elijah ruminated on his situation, the worse he felt. And the worse he felt, the more he ran, until he was consumed by a cave of darkness. He lost sight of the truth and fixated on the false.

The fact is that Elijah was *not* the only faithful one left in Israel.

When the Lord called Elijah out of the cave and gave him his new assignment, God told him he was going to spare "seven thousand in Israel—all whose knees have not bowed down to Baal and whose mouths have not kissed him" (1 Kings 19:18). There were plenty of other faithful people—at least 6,999. But when Elijah's rumination-soaked emotions took control, exaggeration kicked in.

We all struggle with this. When we're in distress, we slide into emotional conclusions that distort or exaggerate the facts. We focus on our feelings, not the objective data. We blame ourselves for things that aren't our fault. We exaggerate the negative. We feel alone and isolated—from others as well as God.

Consider if any of the following thoughts have gotten stuck on replay in your mind lately.

- I'll never change. I'm so tired of trying. I give up.
- No one else cares, so why should I? I'm the only one trying here, and I'm exhausted. If no one else cares, neither do I.
- Others don't understand how I feel. They can't. I'm so alone in this. They just don't know what it's like for me—what I'm really dealing with.
- Lord, do you care what I'm dealing with here? I've been praying and asking for help and being patient. But I'm at the breaking point. I'm sorry to disappoint you, but I can't go on.
- Nobody cares about me—not really. If they did, then they wouldn't let me suffer like this.
- I'm so afraid of what could happen. I feel so out of control. Overwhelmed.

- Why did I not see this coming? I should have known things wouldn't work out.
- What did I do to deserve this? This is all my fault. But what could I have done differently?
- I'm just not strong enough. I can't keep pushing through anymore.
- There's no one I can talk to who will understand. I'm so alone in this.

Any of these sound familiar? But do you also notice how extreme, emotion-based, and exaggerated these are? Recognizing our ruts of rumination is one part of the solution.

Thinking better thoughts based on truth is the other.

Chew or Choose

With the free will God gave us, we can make other choices, ones based on truth, instead of chewing the same old thoughts regardless of how we might feel. Simply put, don't chew your thoughts. *Choose* your thoughts. I'm not saying this is easy, but I am saying it's important. And it does work in diminishing the power rumination has to tilt us toward depression.

At first glance, God's Word explicitly tells us what to do: "Finally, brothers and sisters, whatever is true, whatever is noble, whatever is right, whatever is pure, whatever is lovely, whatever is admirable—if anything is excellent or praiseworthy—think about such things. . . . And the God of peace will be with you" (Philippians 4:8–9). But notice there are a lot of conditions in order to experience the peace promised here!

Changing our thoughts is doable and produces wonderful results. It's not easy but always effective in the battle to leave our caves. Because we will never change our life until we change the way we think.[3] Jesus said, "Then you will know the truth, and the truth will set you free" (John 8:32).

So how does the truth set us free from ruminating? By reminding us what's really going on and replacing old lies with eternal truths. By equipping us to handle the battle before we get lost in a barrage of false assumptions, self-contempt, and negative exaggeration.

The Bible calls this battle demolishing our strongholds: "Though we live in the world, we do not wage war as the world does. The weapons we fight with are not the weapons of the world. On the contrary, they have divine power to demolish strongholds" (2 Corinthians 10:3–4). The Greek word translated here as *strongholds* is *ochyroma* (okh-oo'-ro-mah), which means a castle or fortress. As Paul uses it, it refers to someone held captive by deception.[4] What I like to call incarceration by rumination.

The enemy's greatest game plan is to get you locked down by deception. His greatest tool is a lie: making you believe something untrue has power over you. Jesus said, "When [the devil] lies, he speaks his native language, for he is a liar and the father of lies" (John 8:44). Because we know his strategy is always based on deception, we also know how to win the battle against his strongholds: "We demolish arguments and every pretension that sets itself up against the knowledge of God, and we take captive every thought to make it obedient to Christ" (2 Corinthians 10:5).

This weapon of truth reverberates throughout Scripture: "Do not conform to the pattern of this world, but be transformed by the renewing of your mind" (Romans 12:2). We also see it in the contrast between who we used to be and who we are in Christ: "You were taught . . . to put off your old self, which is being corrupted by its deceitful desires; to be made new in the attitude of your minds" (Ephesians 4:22–23).

We defeat the enemy by replacing every lie with the truth of God's Word. And changing your thinking won't happen by itself—you need a game plan. Otherwise, you'll get worn down by the battle and end up stuck in place—again. At some point, you must draw a line and make a declaration.

From this moment on, I'm fighting back.

My thinking is going to be different—grounded by truth, anchored by faith.

Daily Declarations

When I catch myself slipping into destructive rumination, I use God's truth to pull out the weeds and nourish the soil of my beliefs. I do this by writing out what I call "daily declarations" based on the promises in God's Word. These statements reflect the truth about who God says I am, and they help me remember what I need to do to become the person God has made me to be. For example, *I am disciplined. Christ in me is stronger than the wrong desires in me. I wake up with purpose, direction, and meaning every day of my life.*

Basically, whatever you say to yourself is impressed deeper into your subconscious mind. This means that the more you dwell on the truth, the more truth grows, which leaves less and less room for lies and negativity.

I encourage you to write out your own declarations and read them each morning, maybe even several times a day, and especially when your emotions spill over or cloud your perspective. As you express your own daily declarations, here are a few things to keep in mind:

- Write the declarations in the present tense. Declare who you are in Christ even if you're not feeling it or living it out the way you want. This will motivate you toward believing it and achieving it.

- Create declarations that confront the negative inner voices (the lies you believe, the inadequacies, uncertainties, and emotional conclusions). Keep the declarations positive.
- Make the declarations about yourself and God. Don't make declarations that require others to do anything to change or make you happy.
- Focus on your God-given dreams and calling. Keep your purpose in mind as you craft your declarations.
- Read these statements every day. Revise and add to your list as you grow.

I include my daily declarations as part of my morning devotions. Inspired by my friend Craig Groeschel, I focus on my identity in Christ and my calling as a husband, father, grandfather, friend, pastor, and leader. Here's what my declarations are right now:

- Jesus Christ is the Lord of my life, and I exist to serve and glorify him. I am growing closer to him, and he is giving me supernatural blessing, influence, anointing, and protection.
- Today, my words, thoughts, and imaginations are under the power of Christ. I take all thoughts captive and make them obedient to Christ.
- I am disciplined. Christ in me is stronger than the wrong desires in me. I wake up with purpose, direction, and meaning every day of my life.
- I love my wife and will lay down my life to serve her.
- I love my children and lead them to love God and serve him with their whole hearts. I nurture, equip, train, and empower them to do more for his kingdom than they can imagine.

- I love people and believe the best about them.
- I am called to reach people far from God and take people on a spiritual journey to know God, find freedom, discover purpose, and make a difference.
- I am called to equip leaders and help the church reach her full potential.
- I am called to invest my life in the next generation and empower them to do more than my generation ever did.
- I bring my best today. The world will be different and better because I served Jesus today.
- Today, I love God, love people, pursue excellence, and choose joy.
- I live to make Jesus famous and to give all the glory to God alone.

Write your own declarations or start with these and make them your own. The key is focusing on God's truth and dispelling the enemy's lies. Rumination muddies the water of your thinking and obscures what's true about you. Daily declarations can help you purify and cleanse your thoughts, providing a clearer perspective.

And seeing clearly again, you discover the next step out of your depression.

CHAPTER 7

Social Distancing

The most terrible poverty is loneliness
and the feeling of being unloved.
—MOTHER TERESA

We all remember the coronavirus outbreak in the spring of 2020 and its impact on virtually every area of our lives. We remember words and phrases such as "pandemic," "flattening the curve," "mitigating the disease," and "sheltering in place." Each day we received a new lesson in how to live in a world with contagious disease. Medical terms and procedures became mainstream jargon.

But one pandemic-related term troubled me right away: *social distancing*. From the first time I heard it, I sensed it was misaligned with what healthcare officials intended to communicate. They tried to promote physical separation and self-isolation of individuals in both private and public spaces in order to limit contact and thereby slow the spread of the virus. Recommendations from government officials included avoiding close contact with people who were sick and keeping distance between yourself and other people.

I know they meant well, but I wish the catchphrase had been "physical distancing" rather than "social distancing." Certainly in the interest of promoting health and limiting exposure, being quarantined and keeping at least six feet away from others made sense. But it's possible to maintain physical separation while still remaining socially connected.

In fact, social closeness becomes even more important in times when we're physically separated from one another. Social connections are the building blocks of human life. We need closeness and relationships. Without relationships we wither and fail to thrive. As I pastor, I immediately feared that this preventive recommendation would not only isolate us physically but mentally and psychologically as well.

To defeat depression and come out of our caves, we need each other more than ever.

All by Myself

You see, the first problem mentioned in the Bible wasn't sin—it was isolation. Before Adam and Eve rebelled against God by eating the forbidden fruit, God recognized a problem shortly after he created man—just one man. Everything God had created was good, but seeing his solitary image bearer, God said, "It is not good for the man to be alone" (Genesis 2:18). So God created a female image bearer suitable to be Adam's companion.

Long after the first man and first woman exited Eden, others continued to recognize the perils of isolation. King Solomon had everything—wealth, wisdom, and a very large family—yet he still battled feelings of loneliness. Likely referring to himself, Solomon wrote, "There was a man all alone; he had neither son nor brother. There was no end to his toil, yet his eyes were not content with his wealth" (Ecclesiastes 4:8).

Being isolated wasn't good then, and it still isn't good today.

We experienced social distancing long before the COVID-19 outbreak. Many experts believe ours is the loneliest society in human history. The possibility we could be lonelier than ever seems odd considering the billions of people on the planet and the advancements in technology that connect us globally. Our reality, though, illustrates the truth of our isolation.

Although we're connected in ways no other human beings have been via all manner of digital technologies, those connections can be far from "social." While various platforms allow us to trade pictures, exchange opinions, and share more information, people remain lonelier than ever. Why? *Because we are made for direct human contact.*

And even though the original goal of social media was to connect us and facilitate our need for interaction, it has also created a phenomenon known as "Facebook depression," a malaise afflicting people who spend too much time "engaging" with others online. We distract our minds, delude our hearts, and distance our bodies by relating through screens that will always limit our ability to bond, connect, and belong.

Online relating, even with three-dimensional virtual reality, is not the same as sitting across from someone and having a conversation. Not the same as holding hands as you walk through the park. Not the same as reading a story to a child by your side at bedtime.

There is a big difference in quantity and quality between relating online and relating in person. I experienced this intensely in the first months of COVID lockdown. I seemed to swim harder each day in a sea of endless Zoom meetings, livestream events, and texts. I often felt overwhelmed and worried about the quantity of my social interactions and online connections versus their quality. Ironically, there were days I remember telling my wife that I was "peopled out," feeling too tired to engage with her and our family, the people I love most. And that's the problem. When we invest our relational, social, and emotional energy online, we end up with very little return.

And then wonder why we feel so lonely.

Better Together

Social media and online interactions aside, we all know what it feels like to be alone in a crowd. Sometimes we experience a sense of isolation and not belonging even when we're with family and friends. Both are normal experiences, but they can also push us closer to our cave of depression if left unchecked. When we feel lonely and isolated, we're at greater risk for withdrawing even more.

That seems to be what happened to Elijah in the midst of his struggle. We're told, "When he came to Beersheba in Judah, *he left his servant there*" (1 Kings 19:3, emphasis added). Perhaps feeling overwhelmed by fear, uncertainty, doubt, and despair, Elijah may have concluded it was best to deal with his issues on his own. Maybe he wanted time to process what was going on inside him—to sort himself out, as my British friends like to say.

He may have thought he needed solitude, but what Elijah experienced was isolation. Not long after leaving his servant behind, we're told in the very next verse, Elijah felt like he wanted to die. Alone with the panicked voices in his head, he had no one who could reason with him or remind him of what was true. And so he retreated to the darkness of the cave and hid from reality.

Isolation can be so dangerous because we begin to "counsel" ourselves, ruminating on causes and contributors to our depression, looking for points of light in the darkness but turning away when a spark of hope flickers.

Unfortunately, you're the last person you should listen to when you're isolated and struggling. Some studies show that our IQ drops, perhaps as much as thirty points, when we're isolated or even when we perceive that we're cut off from significant relationships.[1] Apparently, it doesn't take long for isolation to raise our level of cortisol, the stress hormone, which in turn contributes to depression. Increased cortisol also signals our fight-flight-freeze instincts, which can render us more vulnerable to a panic attack, especially if we're ruminating in isolation.

Simply put, it's not good for you to be isolated.

You and I are wired to need relationships. Family. Friends. People who share different facets of our lives. We need people especially when we're struggling because they can provide other perspectives that remind us what's true. They can protect and defend us when we're vulnerable and weak. In his reflection on relationships, Solomon noted, "A person *standing alone* can be attacked and *defeated*, but *two* can stand back-to-back and *conquer. Three* are even *better*, for a triple-braided cord is not easily broken" (Ecclesiastes 4:12 NLT, emphasis added).

God never meant for us to handle life on our own.

We're made for relationships.

We're better together.

We are designed by God for connections and cooperation. We are created for intimacy. We function best in a tribe—a social community linked together by a common bond, to accomplish something none of us could do on our own.

Biblical writers often described the church in communal terms, particularly as a family, united together in facing all life's trials and triumphs: "You should be like one big happy family, full of sympathy toward each other, loving one another with tender hearts and humble minds" (1 Peter 3:8 TLB). The psalmist writes, "God sets the lonely in families" (Psalm 68:6). There are also relational references likening the church to a body (Romans 12:4–5), a fellowship (Acts 2:42), and a flock (John 21:16–17). Clearly, God intends for us to be part of a social and spiritual tribe.

Whether intentionally or incidentally, though, many of us have left our tribes. As a result, we feel cut off from the people we care about most. We know details of others' vacations and big events, but we don't share in them as active participants.

Isolation makes us feel awful. Everything feels heavier when you believe you're the only one carrying the load. Everyone wants to belong and feel needed and wanted. There is no way to function alone and also be fully alive. To function in healthy ways, we have to be fully connected and loved. To be fully connected and loved, we have to be fully known. To be fully known, we have to realize that we need each other.

Foundational to every human being is relational connectedness. With God and with others.

This need never goes away.

Here's the Dirt

This foundational human need for connection is displayed throughout the pages of the Bible, but the most striking example may be how Jesus spent the last night before he was arrested and killed. As the Son of God, we might think Jesus was above needing support from other mere mortals. But Jesus was fully human as well as fully God. Experiencing the fullness of his human experience, he knew the pain of loneliness and he needed companionship just as keenly as we do. During his lowest point, Jesus longed for the support of his closest friends.

After the Passover meal, which we call the Last Supper, Jesus wanted time to pray and reflect on what he was about to face, but he didn't want to be alone, and so he took three of his disciples with him.

Then Jesus went with his disciples to a place called Gethsemane, and he said to them, "Sit here while I go over there and pray." He took Peter and the two sons of Zebedee along with him, and he began to be sorrowful and troubled. Then he said to them, "My soul is overwhelmed with sorrow to the point of death. Stay here and keep watch with me."

Going a little farther, he fell with his face to the ground and prayed, "My Father, if it is possible, may this cup be taken from me. Yet not as I will, but as you will." (Matthew 26:36–39)

In the midst of intense sorrow, knowing the agony of the cross was only hours away, Jesus refused to isolate himself. Even though his disciples would fall asleep in his hour of need and later deny even knowing him, Christ relied on his closest friends. I suspect he knew temptation would be greater if he were by himself. After all, the devil waited until after Jesus had fasted and prayed in the desert for forty days before tempting him with everything in his arsenal.

Perhaps an even more striking demonstration of Jesus' commitment to his relationships is what he had done earlier that evening. As they gathered to celebrate Passover meal together, Jesus astounded these men who knew him best by putting a towel around his waist and washing their feet. Keep in mind two facts about such an intimate act of hospitality. First, people walked everywhere, often barefoot or in sandals, so their feet were filthy by the end of the day—dusty, grimy, sweaty, and, yes, smelly. Second, servants were the only people who washed the feet of others.

By performing this act of up-close-and-personal service, Jesus demonstrated extreme humility and love. Shocked as they were, the disciples were also very uncomfortable. We see this when one of them initially refused: "'No,' said Peter, 'you shall never wash my feet'" (John 13:8).

Had we been there, I suspect our response might have been the same. Peter reacted as many of us often react—by keeping the worst parts of his life to himself. Feet are the lowest part of our body and represent the dirty, cracked, stinky parts of our lives. Peter was not about to allow the perfect and holy Son of God to wash his feet. It was simply too embarrassing and shameful.

We often put up similar defenses when others try to come alongside us in the messiness of our mistakes, secrets, and hardships. Although we're wired to need others, we resist going below the surface and being transparent. It's too vulnerable and needy, too raw and painful. We'd much rather keep our dirty feet hidden inside designer shoes than allow others to see us barefoot.

But Jesus made it clear this isn't an option. He said to Peter, "Unless I wash you, you have no part with me" (John 13:8). Basically, he said that if we keep the worst to ourselves then we'll miss out on the best. Vulnerability and transparency are required for intimacy to flourish—not only with the Lord, who already knows us better than we know ourselves, but also with each other. "We are many parts of one body," wrote the apostle Paul, "and we all belong to each other" (Romans 12:5 NLT).

The truth is, we need each other—dirty feet and all.

The Benefits of Needing People

When we examine the conversation Jesus had with his disciples that night before his death, we find several benefits of healthy relationships. Their conversation is spread over five chapters in John's gospel—chapters 13 through 17—and each chapter reveals a principle relevant to our relationships today.

WE NEED PEOPLE WHO CARE FOR US

Jesus makes this principle clear after washing the disciples' feet:

> When he had finished washing their feet, he put on his clothes and returned to his place. "Do you understand what I have done for you?" he asked them. "You call me 'Teacher' and 'Lord,' and rightly so, for that is what I am. Now that I, your Lord and Teacher, have washed your feet, you also should wash one another's feet. I have set you an example that you should do as I have done for you." (John 13:12–15)

Demonstrating the extent of his humility in service to others, Jesus wanted to make sure his followers got the point. He was encouraging his disciples to follow his example of caring for other people. Knowing he would not be with them much longer, Jesus wanted them to serve each other, even in something as intimate and basic as washing feet.

Today, we live in a self-care society. We're responsible for our own needs and can hire someone if we need help. Consequently, many of us don't like to admit that we need care—real care, genuine compassion demonstrated by actions, attitudes, and words. Needing care leaves us feeling indebted. We worry that others might take advantage of us somehow in the vulnerability of our need. We fear they may see us as weak, dependent, helpless.

But receiving and giving care is at the heart of Christianity. Jesus said the world will know us by our love for one another (John 13:35). We need to be care-givers as well as care-receivers. The wisdom writer put it this way, "It's better to have a partner than go it alone. Share the work, share the wealth. And if one falls down, the other helps, but if there's no one to help, tough!" (Ecclesiastes 4:9–10 THE MESSAGE).

When we get bad news, we need people in our life who will care for us. Paul told us, "Rejoice with those who rejoice; mourn with those who mourn" (Romans 12:15). Because we're connected and doing life together, we care about what happens to one another. "If one part suffers, every part suffers with it; if one part is honored, every part rejoices with it" (1 Corinthians 12:26).

There are many situations in life that no one should have to face alone. Sitting in the hospital waiting room while a loved one is in surgery. Receiving your own medical test results. Enduring the hours and days following the death of a family member. Aching through that first night after a husband or wife walks out. Losing your job. Getting bad news about the struggles your child is facing.

We weren't designed to be self-sufficient when we're suffering.

We Need People Who Will Encourage Us

The word *encourage* means to lift someone's spirits, to be a breath of fresh air for their sails, the wind beneath their wings. Jesus encouraged his disciples when they were troubled by reminding them of their heavenly future. "Don't let your hearts be troubled," he said, "Trust in God, and trust also in me" (John 14:1 NLT).

We all need encouragement, especially during the challenging times in which we live. I'm convinced we need daily doses to keep us from the pull of gravity exerted by depression. Encouragement can take many forms. It can be as simple as a quick text, a silly meme you know will make someone smile, a verse of Scripture the Holy Spirit compels you to send via e-mail, a call, a Post-it note, a treat, an unexpected visit.

Some people say, "I go to the Lord for my encouragement." But the Bible reminds us, "Encourage one another daily, as long as it is called 'Today,' so that none of you may be hardened by sin's deceitfulness" (Hebrews 3:13). Our spirits are quite impressionable, and certain

SOCIAL DISTANCING

circumstances can leave us feeling fragile and broken. The right conversation or word of encouragement from the right person can change
our direction.

Who encourages you on a regular basis? Whom do you routinely
encourage? We can't make one another happy or snap our fingers to
break the hold depression has on those we care about. But we can
encourage others and lift their spirits by reminding them of our love
and presence in their lives.

We Need People Who Will Partner with Us

If we want to overcome loneliness and isolation, we need people
who will partner with us. One of the keys of healthy relationships is
shared goals. We're designed to do something productive together.
This is also one of the keys of overcoming loneliness. Being productive
by contributing to something bigger than ourselves provides a natural
context in which we can care for others.

Jesus told his followers, "Remain in me, as I also remain in you.
No branch can bear fruit by itself; it must remain in the vine. Neither
can you bear fruit unless you remain in me. I am the vine; you are
the branches. If you remain in me and I in you, you will bear much
fruit; apart from me you can do nothing" (John 15:4–5). Basically, he
made it clear that we have to be connected to him as our life source,
but this connection also extends to one another. This biblical principle of teamwork reminds us that the whole is greater than the sum
of its parts.

Because we get way more done if we do it together. The wisdom
writer asserted, "Two are better than one, because they have a good
return for their labor" (Ecclesiastes 4:9). This is not just spiritual truth
but one of the most important principles of teamwork. Or think of it
this way: 1 + 1 = 3, or even more. If you want to accomplish something
bigger and better, you will need to partner with others.

101

WE NEED PEOPLE WHO WILL PROTECT US

Partners also help us see our blind spots because most of us are one step away from doing something stupid on any given day. We need others who can protect us by watching out for our souls. Jesus charged us with helping each other follow his example: "All this I have told you so that you will not *fall away* (John 16:1, emphasis added). We're committed to one another's growth, and this includes guarding each other when we're in danger of messing up. The Greek word translated *away* is *skandalizo*, and it means both a snare and a scandal, which have a lot in common.

I like to say Jesus introduced the first "neighborhood watch" program! But, seriously, think about it. We keep our eyes open while our neighbors are away on vacation—how much more important to watch out for their souls? Instead of organizing a neighborhood watch for our property and possessions, we need neighbors who will look out for our spiritual health.

Who is doing that for you? Who has your back spiritually?

You and I have a very real enemy who is relentless in pursuing our downfall.

Every day he is setting snares in our paths. He's waiting for us to turn our backs so he can attack our blind spots. He's usually most successful when we're fighting on our own. The wisdom of Scripture is, "A person standing alone can be attacked and defeated, but two can stand back-to-back and conquer. Three are even better, for a triple-braided cord is not easily broken" (Ecclesiastes 4:12 NLT).

When you're back-to-back with someone, you see 180 degrees in one direction while they see 180 in the other. Together, you have the full 360 and can see and preempt attacks before they do much damage. When someone's got your back, they protect you by seeing what you cannot see.

Sometimes we can cover each other's blind spots by asking the right questions. I love the spiritual assessment devised by John Wesley, the founding father of Methodists and a major proponent of small groups. He encouraged members of his congregation to question one another on a weekly basis in order to prevent temptation, facilitate confession, and hasten forgiveness. Modern pastors such as Chuck Swindoll have adopted Wesley's method and suggested questions such as:[2]

- Have you been in a compromising situation this week?
- Have any of your financial dealings lacked integrity?
- Have you viewed any sexually explicit material?
- Have you spent quality time in Bible study and prayer?
- Have you given priority time to your family?
- Have you fulfilled the mandates of your calling?
- Have you just lied to me?

Don't you love it? These questions set aside polite niceties to get right to the point. They do an end run on potential snares by exposing them before we trip into them.

Who's asking you the tough questions—about where you go, who you see, and what you do when no one else is looking?

Similarly, to whom are you posing tough questions? Whose back do you have? When was the last time you told someone, "I'm with you through thick or thin," or "We'll get through this together"?

We Need People Who Will Pray for Us

God didn't design you to be the only one who prays for yourself. Jesus modeled praying for one another throughout his ministry. He also modeled being specific about those we pray for. "After Jesus said this, he looked toward heaven and prayed. . . . 'I pray for them. I am not praying for the world, but for those you have given me'" (John 17:1, 9). Jesus knew his disciples needed spiritual covering for protection and provision. We do the same thing when we pray for the people in our lives. Our prayers create a shield to cover them and help them through each day. "Prayer is essential in this ongoing warfare," wrote the apostle Paul, "Pray hard and long. Pray for your brothers and sisters" (Ephesians 6:18 THE MESSAGE).

Throughout my life, I've been blessed by the prayers of those who committed to interceding for me. These are people who know me well, who share my faith, and who cover me, my family, and my ministry in continual prayer. I confide in them and trust them to pray according to what's going on.

We all need this type of covering.

All it takes is honesty and communication.

Don't be afraid to ask.

Because if we're going to win the battle against loneliness and isolation, we need authentic relationships to guide and sustain us. Like Moses, we need an Aaron and a Hur to hold up our arms.

Perhaps you remember the story in Exodus 17. The Israelites were encountering their first major opposition from the Amalekites. While Joshua led the Israelites into battle, Moses, along with Aaron and Hur, watched from a nearby hill. Sounds like they were merely spectators until you realize the power they wielded from a distance: "As long as Moses held up his hands, the Israelites were winning, but whenever he lowered his hands, the Amalekites were winning" (Exodus 17:11).

When Moses became weary, Aaron and Hur supported him by holding up his arms until the Israelites were able to finally defeat the Amalekites. Moses could part the Red Sea but couldn't hold up his own arms!

We are all called to hold up each other's arms—to support one another. Because sooner or later, we all get tired. We get weary and discouraged. We get sick or injured. We lose a loved one. We get fired. We fall and need help getting up again.

Who's holding up your arms?

CHAPTER 8

Rainy Days and Mondays

It's not what happens *to* me that matters but
what happens *in* me that matters most.
—John Maxwell

I don't remember how old I was, but I know exactly how I felt the first time I heard Karen Carpenter sing "Rainy Days and Mondays." And yes, they always got me down.

I was in elementary school and riding the school bus home. It had been a lousy day for reasons I can't recall—probably a low grade on a math quiz along with rejection at recess from my latest crush. Overcast skies bruised by the rumble of thunder finally opened just as the bell rang. Without a jacket or umbrella, I stood in line outside waiting for the bus along with dozens of classmates, all of us getting soaked.

Collapsing into the first vacant seat, I felt like it was the perfect ending to a perfectly terrible day. I was tired, drenched, and ready for that first day of a new week to end. Then suddenly, there was that voice, low and beautiful, the soundtrack of my sadness coming from a radio somewhere. Karen Carpenter expressing exactly how I felt with details uncanny in their accuracy. It *was* a rainy Monday. I was every bit a lonely clown with a frown. How did she know?

Somehow, hearing that song gave me comfort. As alone as I felt in my sodden misery, I realized that everybody must have days like this—or there wouldn't be a popular song about it! Years later, I also realized that while we'll always have Mondays and rainy days, they don't always have to get us down.

Yes, there will always be hard days where nothing seems to go right. When you get a flat while driving to work. Spill coffee down your shirt. Forget to attend the important meeting. Lose your homework. Burn the chicken. However, as we mature, those trivial spills and slips usually don't bother us as much as they once did. We grow up and realize that harder things happen. That life is unpredictable, and even though we try to be ready for it, we're not ever completely ready. No matter how strong our faith, family, values, and support structures may be, circumstances still take a toll on our emotions.

But we don't have to allow circumstances or feelings to dictate our actions.

The Bible says that rain falls on us all, both the righteous and unrighteousness (Matthew 5:45). I'm reminded of the French phrase *c'est la vie*—that's life!—I grew up hearing in Louisiana. Rather than allowing a flat tire to send us into a spiral of despair, we can accept that we ran over a nail in the road, get the flat fixed, and keep going. Events on earth are never going to turn out perfectly—nor has God promised us that they would or should. When he sent Jesus to live as a man and die on the cross for the sins of the world, God implemented the ultimate rescue plan, not a fix-it plan.

Spiritual Vertigo

Exercising our faith in God and maintaining equanimity, which is the ability to see the bigger picture beyond our immediate distress, requires consistent practice. When circumstances are manageable, it's easy to trust God, live out of our purpose, and enjoy our blessings. But it's harder to keep our faith strong when we experience what I call spiritual vertigo.

If you've ever been on top of a building, mountain, or overlook, and gazed down only to feel as if the ground were suddenly rushing up to meet you, you understand the disorienting experience of vertigo. While you don't have to climb great heights to experience it, vertigo leaves you feeling unbalanced, dizzy, and uncertain about depth perception. When suffering from it, some people fall if they turn their head too quickly or rise from a chair. Vertigo can also be caused by an inner ear problem or other issues with how the brain maintains the body's equilibrium.

Spiritual vertigo occurs when our faith is shaken by unexpected circumstances, especially ones in which, like Elijah, we go from great heights to frightening lows in record time. When our lowest lows come on the heels of our highest of highs, we feel confused, untethered, and disoriented by the descent.

Spiritual vertigo describes why Sunday nights have so often left me feeling empty, exhausted, and emotionally dizzy after experiencing the exuberance of ministering so intensely that weekend. It also accounts for Elijah's rapid descent from mighty prophet of God to suicidal cave dweller. Elijah was probably getting ready to host a party to celebrate the success of defeating the prophets of Baal. And then the bad news came: Queen Jezebel wanted to kill him. Just like that, the joy of seeing God's dramatic display of power collapsed into a clutter of overwhelming emotions—fear, dread, uncertainty, and despair.

On the other end of the spectrum, we find the apostle Paul. If anyone had earned the right to share the secret of abiding peace and joy regardless of circumstances, it had to be Paul (Philippians 4:11–12). Repeatedly, he avoided the distress and depression of dire circumstances—arrests, beatings, shipwrecks, snakebites, and imprisonment—by relying on his faith in God (2 Corinthians 1:8–11). Paul's example reveals how we, too, can find joy in the middle of hard times (2 Corinthians 4:8–10; 11:23–29).

No matter what he experienced, Paul kept his faith and remained confident in the power of the Holy Spirit. I'm especially impressed by Paul's letter, written while he was imprisoned in Rome, to the community of Jesus-followers in Philippi. In this letter, Paul repeatedly uses the words *joy* and *rejoice*.

What was Paul's secret? Let's take a closer look.

More Than Happiness

Paul had planted this church in the city of Philippi during his second missionary journey to ports along the Mediterranean Sea. A coastal city in the rugged, hilly region overlooking the bay near Neapolis, Philippi became the first recorded Christian congregation in Europe, dating to AD 50–52. More than a decade later, around AD 62, Paul was in Rome, literally chained to a soldier of the Roman Empire, awaiting execution for preaching the gospel of Christ.

Despite enduring the injustice of this incarceration for two years, Paul's focus remained on ministry. He wanted to encourage believers in Philippi who might also be experiencing persecution and imprisonment. So this is how Paul started his letter:

> I thank my God every time I remember you. In all my prayers for all of you, I always pray with joy because of your partnership in the gospel from the first day until now, being confident of this, that he who began a good work in you will carry it on to completion until the day of Christ Jesus. (Philippians 1:3–6)

After two years of imprisonment, what was the first thing Paul did? He thanked God and expressed concern for others! I have to be honest and admit that's not where my mind and attention would be if I were in his place. Perhaps you would admit the same. When life seems unfair and our circumstances confine us, most of us struggle to pray, let alone give thanks to God.

Paul's message clearly wasn't just polite lip service either. He reported that he *always* prayed with joy and remained confident that God's good work in the Philippians would continue and be completed—even as his own plans had been thwarted and derailed. How could Paul have been so encouraging despite his own difficult situation?

Paul had found something more powerful than mere happiness. His faith anchored him in an unshakable joy that went so much deeper than what you and I usually consider happiness. So many of us pursue happiness as our life's goal, and happiness isn't bad. But we tend to tie our happiness to events and circumstances, all of which can change in an instant. Abiding joy, on the other hand, has its basis in something that never changes. As Paul continued his letter, notice how he revealed the source of lasting spiritual joy:

> And this is my prayer: that your love may abound more and more in *knowledge* and *depth of insight*, so that you may be able to discern what is best and may be pure and blameless for the day of Christ, filled with the fruit of righteousness that comes through Jesus Christ—to the glory and praise of God. (Philippians 1:9–11, emphasis added)

Most striking here, at least to me, is that Paul *didn't question God* about what was going on in his life. His focus remained on what he had in Christ, not what he lacked circumstantially. I would look through those prison bars and wonder, *Did I miss something, Lord?*

Where are you? Why are you allowing this to happen? Paul kept an eternal perspective, allowing the hope of heaven to clarify his purpose, not his temporary, earthly circumstances.

After questioning God, I'd probably start looking for someone else to blame, as so many of us do when circumstances crash. When we blame others, though, we give up the power we have to change. Carl Rogers, a pioneering twentieth-century psychologist said, "The only person who cannot be helped is the person who blames others."[1] Accepting responsibility—not for what happened to us but for our response to it—is essential for exercising faith and sustaining spiritual joy.

Paul could easily have focused on being falsely accused and sentenced to death. He could have obsessed about his dirty, dank cell and the terrible food he received occasionally. He could have complained about being chained to someone watching his every move.

But Paul didn't complain about anything.

Instead, he chose to look beyond the distraction of his painful circumstances (2 Corinthians 4:16–18). He refused to doubt what he knew was true eternally because of the discomfort he experienced temporarily. Short-term suffering could not shake his bedrock faith in God's power, promises, and goodness. His jail term didn't have to make sense to him because Paul knew God ultimately had things under control—no matter how out of control he might have felt at times.

Don't Ask Why

Some people never seem to get over their disappointment when things go wrong. They continually analyze events from all angles in search of some kind of reason that will explain what happened to them. Others stop trusting God because they falsely believe he's obligated to make their lives work the way they want.

They forget that Jesus told us that we could count on problems in this life: "In this world you will have trouble. But take heart! I have overcome the world" (John 16:33). Notice that we can have peace through Christ not because we don't have problems—he acknowledges we *will* have trouble in this world, but because he has overcome the world. Therefore, we're missing the point when we get hung up on asking "Why?" about every adversity that comes our way. The hope of heaven is the ultimate promise that everything works out in the end. Frequently, we slip into the mind-set that when we trust God, he's obligated to make life work the way we want it to work. But in this world, we're guaranteed to face problems. In the next, however, we will experience only the joy and peace of heaven. Sometimes we must lower our expectations of what's possible in this life on earth.

In fact, one of the most liberating truths I've ever learned is that my problems are not a measure of my spirituality. The strength of my faith does not depend on having a worry-free, stress-free life. In fact, just the opposite! Everyone has problems. We all have good days and bad days. When I want to be the exception and am tempted to feel sorry for myself, I think of something else Paul shared.

In a letter to the believers in Corinth, Paul revealed his chronic struggle with what he identified as a "thorn in my flesh" (2 Corinthians 12:6–7). He prayed for God to remove the cause of his suffering three times before he got an answer—and it wasn't the answer he had hoped to receive.

> But he said to me, "My grace is sufficient for you, for my power is made perfect in weakness." Therefore I will boast all the more gladly about my weaknesses, so that Christ's power may rest on me. That is why, for Christ's sake, I delight in weaknesses, in insults, in hardships, in persecutions, in difficulties. For when I am weak, then I am strong. (vv. 9–10)

Instead of sinking into disappointment, rebelling, or withdrawing from God, Paul trusts the One he serves. Paul doesn't roll out the "Why?" slide leading into a cave of depression. He knew that if his plans didn't work out that God was doing something far better. And that is evidenced in his message to the Philippians: "Now I want you to know, brothers and sisters, that what has happened to me has actually served to advance the gospel" (Philippians 1:12).

Instead of asking, "Why did this happen to me?" Paul asks a better question: "How can I serve?" When circumstances don't go as planned, we have to look for other opportunities. When he was no longer free to travel and preach, Paul decided to write letters instead. And in so doing, he made a major contribution to the Bible! Instead of dwelling on why his original plan hadn't worked out, Paul focused on doing what he could do.

Instead of preaching to hundreds or thousands of listeners, Paul focused on those he still could influence, particularly while chained to a rotation of prison guards. And here's what happened:

> As a result, it has become clear throughout the whole palace guard and to everyone else that I am in chains for Christ. And because of my chains, most of the brothers and sisters have become confident in the Lord and dare all the more to proclaim the gospel without fear. (Philippians 1:13–14)

Paul preached to every person chained to him, and consequently the whole palace guard learned about Jesus. When Paul couldn't preach to a huge crowd, he saw an opportunity he still had, and he took it.

We need to do the same.

Instead of "Why me, Lord?" we need to ask, "What can I do for you, Lord?" Or, "What would you like to teach me?" Pivoting from "Why?" to "What?" changes our perspective. When we see our circumstances differently, our attitude often changes as well. Rather than wander in the dark cave of depression, we follow God even when we can see only the next step in front of us. Joy is an attitude that trusts God in all circumstances. Which is why Paul could say, "We know that in all things God works for the good of those who love him, who have been called according to his purpose" (Romans 8:28).

So What?

Once we shift perspective and change our attitude, we learn to refocus on what really matters. Paul received word that other ministries were springing up. Some people were complaining and trying to put Paul in the middle of controversy and contention. They started church rivalries and questioned each other's motives. In his response, though, it's clear Paul refused to play their games:

> It is true that some preach Christ out of envy and rivalry, but others out of goodwill. The latter do so out of love, knowing that I am put here for the defense of the gospel. The former preach Christ out of selfish ambition, not sincerely, supposing that they can stir up trouble for me while I am in chains. But *what does it matter*? The important thing is that in every way, whether from false motives or true, Christ is preached. And because of this I *rejoice*. Yes, and I will continue to *rejoice*. (Philippians 1:15–18, emphasis added)

The Greek phrase translated here as "what does it matter" is *tis gar plen*,[2] which could also be translated as, "So what?" Paul asked a question that continues to be a tool for our discernment in the midst of challenging circumstances: "What difference does it really make what happens?" He's reminding us of a fundamental lesson on experiencing real joy. Does this circumstance have an impact on eternity? Or does it have an expiration date that will soon pass? Will this matter a hundred years from now? Does it have significance in light of eternity? Is this urgent right now but inconsequential tomorrow or next year or ten years from now?

In our family no one has exemplified this *tis gar plen* approach to life better than Tammy's grandmother, known to our family as Ma Maw Hornsby. Whenever she saw anyone pouting or down in the dumps, she would say, "You've got the world by the tail!" Her meaning was clear: *Keep your perspective and count your blessings.* In fact, this was her motto for living.

Ma Maw had another favorite response that she made popular in our family long before certain TV characters made it popular: "Fuhgeddaboudit!" I don't know where she picked it up or why it stuck, but any time something went wrong or anyone got frustrated or disappointed, she'd say it. Hearing her run her words together and raise her eyebrows always took the focus off our problem, restored perspective, and made us laugh.

Ma Maw's son Billy, who is my father-in-law, once told a story about skipping school when he was a boy. When he didn't show up for classes, his teacher notified the local truancy agent, who called Billy's mom. When she heard Billy skipped school that day, Ma Maw laughed and told the agent, "Well, everybody needs a day off once in a while!" Not the response of most parents, then or now!

When you have Ma Maw's perspective, few things in life can bother you for long. Today's disappointment or tomorrow's tragedy lose their power to rob you of your joy. You can endure hurricanes, pandemics, unemployment, and health crises without losing sight of who God is.

You can even face death without fear.

The Hope of Heaven

Throughout his life, Paul frequently faced death threats. When Jewish religious leaders and Roman officials threatened him with prison, Paul basically shrugged and didn't resist arrest. As we've seen, he used the time in prison to preach through writing rather than speaking. After his release Paul received warnings that his persecutors would send him back. I can imagine his response might have been something like, "Great—I'd love to finish writing those letters I started. In fact, can I go back there? Because I really loved ministering to the guards and jailer."

When his adversaries threatened to kill him, Paul refused to let any circumstance rule his life: "Christ will be exalted in my body, whether by life or death. For to me, to live is Christ and to die is gain" (Philippians 1:20–21). He was unfazed by worst-case scenarios because he had Jesus, which meant no matter what happened, Paul won. If he remained alive, he would serve the Lord and preach the message of Christ. If he died, then he would be with God in heaven. It was the ultimate win-win! No threat could intimidate him, scare him, or bully him.

We can know the same peace and freedom from the turmoil of changing circumstances—even when facing death. I think of my father's battle with cancer and how so many people, thousands around the world, prayed for his healing and recovery—which the Lord granted, just not the way we had hoped. Dad left this life to experience perfect wholeness and eternal joy with God. Knowing that my dad had lived a life based on Paul's win-win attitude, we put this verse on his memorial program: "The Lord will rescue me from every evil attack and will bring me safely to his heavenly kingdom. To him be glory for ever and ever. Amen" (2 Timothy 4:18).

So often we keep hoping for a better now, when sometimes God's solution is a better place. When we know God created us for a reason, we can live fully and trust him each step of the way—regardless of our circumstances. When we accept the gift of salvation through Jesus and know his Holy Spirit dwells within us, we have the peace of knowing where we will spend eternity. Our security cannot change based on painful circumstances or terrible events. We still deal with the emotions—I was devastated to lose my father even though I have great peace and comfort knowing I'll see him again someday in heaven.

But no matter how much our hearts ache, we can continue to trust the author and finisher of our faith, the Creator who designed us and the Father who loved us enough to send his only Son to die on the cross for our sins. We can enjoy the security of his win-win solution—for eternity!

The hope of heaven is a sure thing when you've accepted God's grace. It is a hope from which we draw comfort when faced with trials and tough times. I remember as a kid visiting my maternal grandparents in Louisiana and going with them to their little country church. The services were good but even better were what they called "singings." Twenty to thirty of us would show up in this little one-room church and sing all the old hymns and gospel songs. My dad played the piano, which always needed tuning, but no one seemed to mind. We'd sit around singing for hours.

After attending a few of these singings, I noticed that many of the songs were about heaven. "Some glad morning, when this life is over, I'll fly away," we'd sing. Or, "When we all get to heaven, what a day of rejoicing that will be." We had "blessed assurance" and "peace like a river" because "when the roll is called up yonder, I'll be there."

Today, many of the praise and worship songs I hear focus on asking God to respond in the here and now. There's nothing wrong with that, and God certainly moves here on earth—after all, he sent Jesus with an ultimate rescue plan. A plan to rescue us from what we deserve for our sins and all the pain, sorrow, suffering, worry, anxiety, and depression we often experience in this fallen world. But it's the hope of heaven that keeps me going when everything else seems to be dragging me toward the darkness of my cave.

Heaven is the ultimate hope.

And that's why when Jesus encouraged people, he never focused on the here and now but on heaven. He told his followers to take comfort in the promise of our heavenly home:

> "Don't let your hearts be troubled. Trust in God, and trust also in me. There is more than enough room in my Father's home. If this were not so, would I have told you that I am going to prepare a place for you? When everything is ready, I will come and get you, so that you will always be with me where I am. And you know the way to where I am going."
>
> "No, we don't know, Lord," Thomas said. "We have no idea where you are going, so how can we know the way?"
>
> Jesus told him, "I am the way, the truth, and the life. No one can come to the Father except through me." (John 14:1–6 NLT)

No matter what you're facing, don't let your heart be troubled. Not because God will fix your circumstances or provide all the answers and take away your pain. But because of heaven. Because you have a glorious home with God for all eternity!

Even with all the craziness in this world, we can know the kind of joy and peace Paul displayed. We know no person or circumstance can take away our joy because we have God's presence in our lives now—and forever. Up to this point, I've assumed you're a Christian reader, but do you have the hope of heaven? Have you given your life to Jesus to pay for your sins? If you haven't or you're not sure, then I urge you to open your heart to him today! Here's a short prayer that you can pray to accept his free gift of salvation and make sure you will spend eternity with him in heaven.

> Jesus, I need you. I know that I am a sinner, and I am sorry for my sins. Forgive me for living my life my way. Today I invite you to be the Lord of my life, and I surrender my life completely to you. Take control of my life and make me the kind of person you want me to be. I believe you are the Son of God. I believe you died, were buried, and rose again. Today I put my faith in you. In your name I pray, amen.

I pray that God helps you with whatever you're facing on earth. I hope you discover real relief from depression as you step out of the darkness. I dare to hope that you find some solutions and helpful practices in this book. But there's nothing stronger than the hope of heaven. And I want you to have that hope.

For those who know God . . .

This is as bad as it gets. It only gets better.

For those who don't know God . . .

This is as good as it gets. It only gets worse.

Don't stay in the dark when you can walk in the light!

CHAPTER 9

The Unseen Enemy

The enemy will not see you vanish into God's
company without an effort to reclaim you.
—C. S. Lewis

W*hat did you say?"* I asked. Surely, what I thought I heard couldn't
be accurate.

"The ophthalmologist said the inflammation in Sarah's eye is serious," Tammy said. "He thinks she might be blind permanently if it
progresses. He even mentioned the possibility of multiple sclerosis."

"Wait a minute—back up, honey. Please walk me through this
again."

My wife sighed and began recounting how our daughter Sarah,
then thirteen, came home from school that day with one of her eyes
terribly irritated and distressed. Tammy had taken her to the pediatrician, who couldn't identify the cause after ruling out a stye or pink eye
and referred Sarah to an eye doctor, who miraculously agreed to see
her right away. After examining our daughter, this doctor delivered the
stunning speculation that shook Tammy and resulted in her call to me.

I was about to lead our Wednesday evening prayer service but promised to be home as soon as I could. We ended our call, and as I mentally replayed everything my wife had just told me, I suddenly had a clear suspicion what was going on. And it had more to do with what was happening in our church than in my daughter's optic nerve.

No Coincidence

When it comes to spiritual warfare, I try not to see a demon behind every bush and have always liked the balanced approach described by C. S. Lewis:

> There are two equal and opposite errors into which our race can fall about the devils. One is to disbelieve in their existence. The other is to believe, and to feel an excessive and unhealthy interest in them. They themselves are equally pleased by both errors and hail a materialist or a magician with the same delight.[1]

But after considering the very conspicuous timing of Sarah's problem, I suspected it was no coincidence and found it hard not to believe the enemy was somehow involved. You see, that day Tammy called was September 4, 2002, and our church was on the verge of hosting our first big public outreach event in less than a week.

A little more than a year old, Church of the Highlands was starting to average almost a thousand in attendance each week. To help our ministry presence grow in the community, we planned a city-wide remembrance service on the first anniversary of the September 11 terrorist attacks. We were already outgrowing our meeting space and decided to rent a big auditorium at Samford University. To publicize the event, we printed flyers and rented billboards. Hoping thousands would attend, we felt led to invest more time, energy, and money in this event than anything our church had done so far. Most of the big pieces were in place, and now it was a matter of prayer and final preparations.

In other words, my focus was consumed by making this event a success—until I learned the potentially serious if not life-changing news about Sarah's eye. Even as I led the prayer service that Wednesday evening, I felt a mixture of competing emotions—fear, anger, frustration, and anxiety over my little girl's health. If the devil wanted to divert my attention from the big outreach event, he chose a target I could not ignore, and rightfully so.

For the next three days, I waffled about what to do—if anything. Of course, I prayed, but my prayers reflected the roller coaster of feelings careening on the track of my faith: "Lord, you know I'll do anything for you and have tried to serve with complete and absolute obedience. I know this outreach service is vitally important for your kingdom in so many ways. But you've also given me this precious family, and now my sweet Sarah is suffering and may go blind. I sense the enemy is somehow involved and pray in the name of Jesus for Sarah's complete healing. Please, God. *Please!*"

Over those three days, a terrible thought had also sprung up like a weed in my mind: *If I back out of the event, then Sarah will be okay. If I don't and give my all to the outreach service, then Sarah will pay the price.* I tried to be rational and tell myself that I was overreacting. But without any improvement in Sarah's eye, I felt the tension continue to build. "Lord, I don't know if I can do this," I prayed. "This is not what I signed up for."

Nevertheless, that Saturday morning, I did my duty and half-heartedly drove to church for a big pre-event meeting to soak the remembrance service in prayer. Pulling up to a notoriously long stop light, I glanced at the passenger seat and saw my Bible. Without thinking, I did something I always warn others not to do and randomly flipped open the Good Book. My eyes immediately landed on a passage that sent a tingle racing down my spine:

"Where, O death, is your victory?
Where, O death, is your sting?"
The sting of death is sin, and the power of sin is the law. But thanks be to God! He gives us the victory through our Lord Jesus Christ.
Therefore, my dear brothers and sisters, stand firm. Let nothing move you. Always give yourselves fully to the work of the Lord, because you know that your labor in the Lord is not in vain."
(1 Corinthians 15:55–58)

My mind whirled while my heart accelerated faster than my car after the light turned green. *"Let nothing move you."* Yes, this was true—we shouldn't fret about our perishable bodies because there is a resurrection—but I still didn't want to see my sweet daughter lose her eyesight, let alone battle MS. The more I reflected on that passage, though, the more I knew I had to trust God completely. In that moment, I made the unbearable choice to reaffirm my commitment to God and serve him no matter what—including the possibility that Sarah might lose her vision, or worse. I would just continue to pray for her and trust God with the results while completing the mission he had given me for the outreach.

Angel from Montgomery

At our Sunday service the next morning, a curious thing happened: I was approached by a dear friend who had just learned about Sarah's eye. "My father is a neurologist in Montgomery," he said. "I know he would be willing to examine Sarah and give you a second opinion."

I thanked him for his kindness but told him I wasn't sure it would help. Still, he insisted, and so Monday morning we drove Sarah to this impromptu appointment, trying not to get our hopes up.

After conducting a thorough exam and an MRI, this doctor told us that the problem with Sarah's optic nerve, which mysteriously had no discernable cause, was indeed serious and could result in permanent blindness. The good news, however, is that he saw no signs whatsoever of MS. When we pressed him on a course of treatment or next steps, he said, "Wait a few days and see if the eye heals on its own. Sometimes these matters correct themselves. If it's not better by the end of the week, call me and we'll make a plan."

We agreed and returned home with his bittersweet diagnosis. I thanked God that Sarah didn't have multiple sclerosis but still begged him to heal her eye completely. While Tammy kept Sarah as comfortable as possible, I proceeded with last-minute details and gave myself wholeheartedly to our outreach event that Wednesday, exactly one year after the unthinkable events of 9/11.

While our mood was somber, reflective, and respectful as befitting such a remembrance service, we also thanked God for his faithfulness and presented the good news of salvation through a personal relationship with Jesus. Thousands of people attended with more than six hundred making decisions to accept Christ! The turnout exceeded our hopes and introduced us and our commitment to serve throughout the region. By all definitions, the event was a tremendous success.

The next morning, Thursday, when Sarah woke up, we noticed her eye no longer seemed to be so swollen and irritated. Nor did it hurt her or prevent her from seeing clearly. It almost seemed to heal overnight! When we had her examined by a doctor again, he could find nothing wrong with her or her vision. Now a healthy young woman, wife, and mother of my grandchildren, Sarah has never had any more problems with her eyes.

I often share this example about Sarah's mysterious eye ailment because it confirms my belief in the unseen spiritual realities taking place around us. If this kind of thing had happened just that one time, I might be tempted to agree with those who'd call it happenstance. But now that I have forty-two years of experience as a Christian and thirty-seven years of experience as a pastor to draw on, I can say with certainty that it's definitely *not* coincidental.

In fact, some calamity, crisis, or major distraction seems to occur just before Easter weekend almost every year, right when we're preparing for record numbers of visitors at multiple services throughout the state. Problems pop up right when my new book releases. An unforeseen conflict arises to create tension during a pastor's conference or holiday outreach. I've seen it happen so often that I've come to expect it.

But don't take my word for it based on these experiences.

God's Word spells it out for us plain and simple. It teaches us that there is another dimension you and I can't see that is always operating around us. It's a spiritual dimension—one the apostle Paul referred to as the "heavenly realms." In this unseen, spiritual dimension, Paul said a war rages. "For our struggle is not against flesh and blood," he wrote, "but against the rulers, against the authorities, against the powers of this dark world and against the spiritual forces of evil in the heavenly realms" (Ephesians 6:12).

This is a battle for your soul. One that can leave you wounded, collapsing in an unfamiliar wilderness, or hiding in a dark cave.

Fight with Light

As we've seen, depression has many components and layers—some biological, chemical, and neurological, and others social, relational, and environmental. In examining all the facets of depression and anxiety, though, I would be remiss not to include attacks from the enemy of your soul. He's out to destroy you. The apostle Peter gave us this warning, "Be alert and of sober mind. Your enemy the devil prowls around like a roaring lion looking for someone to devour" (1 Peter 5:8).

Just as there are physical, emotional, and psychological factors contributing to depression, we must also consider the spiritual factors. Looking at depression through only one lens limits our ability to understand it, treat it, and prevent it. And I fear that too often, we overlook the way the devil works against us in depression.

Once again, I want to be clear that I advocate a holistic and balanced approach. We cannot simply blame our depression, or any other struggle, entirely on the devil. We have responsibility for our choices as well as direct access to God's power for winning our spiritual battles. "The devil made me do it" is not a valid excuse because he can't *make* us do anything. But he does influence our lives.

Spiritual warfare may be new territory for you. Or maybe you've heard the term but haven't taken it seriously. I'm not trying to frighten you or confuse you about how to overcome depression, but I do want to inform you about a real and necessary consideration. Because dismissing or ignoring the enemy's attacks only gives him greater leverage in your life.

At the other extreme, we must not use the reality of demonic attacks as a license or excuse for our own mistakes and weaknesses. When our car runs out of gas on the side of the highway, we might be tempted to blame the "demon of forgetfulness," but the truth is most likely that we're the ones who forgot to fill up the tank. Rarely is spiritual attack immediately obvious, because the enemy likes to sneak up on us if possible. It's a given that he's after you, but he'll do all he can to disguise his presence. Remember, he "masquerades as an angel of light" and his servants "masquerade as servants of righteousness" (2 Corinthians 11:14–15).

We see evidence of this battle in Jesus' earthly ministry. One of his primary missions was to cast out demons. Jesus always addressed people's needs from a spiritual perspective, and that included delivering them from the power of the devil. The Bible tells us, "God anointed Jesus of Nazareth with the Holy Spirit and power, and . . . he went around doing good and healing all who were under the power of the devil, because God was with him" (Acts 10:38).

Prior to Jesus' time on earth, God's people often rebelled against him by worshipping idols. Anytime we shift our focus from the living God and turn our heart toward an object, person, or worldly power, it's idolatry. Throughout the Old Testament, we find numerous occasions when the people of Israel disobeyed God and worshiped objects, such as a golden calf they had crafted themselves, or pagan gods from other tribes and cultures.

Whenever his people committed idolatry, God sent a prophet to warn them and urge repentance, which is the job Elijah was tasked with performing. His mission was complicated by the fact that the king and queen of Israel, Ahab and Jezebel, were themselves fervent idolaters. Thus, the big showdown between Elijah and the prophets of Baal was also a confrontation between God and the spirit of idolatry unleashed by Israel's leaders.

Elijah's story isn't simply one of being on the run from danger. He wasn't running away from Jezebel, leaving his servant behind, collapsing in the wilderness, and hiding in a cave just because his fear overwhelmed him and his faith wavered. Elijah was in a spiritual battle for his soul, his future.

When we face the factors of our depression, we're in the same kind of battle. As uncomfortable as it may make you, the devil is real and he's dead set against you. This enemy is doing everything he can to "steal, kill, and destroy" (John 10:10 CEB). The good news, however, is that every demon in hell bows to the name of Jesus.

Based on the truth of God's Word, let's explore three spiritual realities, three spiritual weapons, and three spiritual practices that can help us fight the enemy's darkness with the light and power of Christ.

Three Spiritual Realities

Here are some spiritual realities we can't deny:

1. THE DEVIL IS REAL

First and foremost, you have to accept the truth about who the devil is and what he's up to. He's not an imaginary figure from fairy tales or mythology, not the grinning cartoon villain with red horns and a pitchfork. If he can undermine your belief in his existence, then he's already gained an advantage. In fact, his greatest trick may be to convince you that he's not real.

According to a survey by George Barna, more than half of American Christians don't believe in a literal devil.[2] But remember, "Satan himself masquerades as an angel of light" (2 Corinthians 11:14). Masquerades involve masks, deception, and hiding what's true. If the devil has a superpower, it's looking like an angel of light when he is, in fact, the prince of darkness.

Such deception makes sense when we consider that Lucifer was first an angel (Ezekiel 28:14–16) who rebelled against God (Isaiah 14:12–15) and was cast out of heaven, along with a third of the angelic hosts who followed him. Sworn to oppose God and thwart his purposes, these fallen angels are now among us on earth:

Then war broke out in heaven. Michael and his angels fought against the dragon, and the dragon and his angels fought back. But he was not strong enough, and they lost their place in heaven.

The great dragon was hurled down—that ancient serpent called the devil, or Satan, who leads the whole world astray. He was hurled to the earth, and his angels with him. (Revelation 12:7–9)

Demons are fallen angels who relish derailing our relationship with God and distracting us from living out our God-given purpose. According to the Bible, demons are seductive, evil, and debilitating. They energize wickedness and cause suffering, illness, and physical distress. Demons are not abstract symbols of evil. They exist along with their master, the devil, and delight in your destruction.

2. The Devil Wants to Destroy You

Jesus identified Satan and described his mission perfectly when he said, "The thief comes only to steal and kill and destroy" (John 10:10). And his efforts are not just a matter of planning a one-time heist that robs us of our joy, peace, and purpose. The devil is always looking for ways to strike, scheming and plotting for ways to exploit us at any and every opportunity. Which is why the apostle Peter admonished us, "Be alert and of sober mind. Your enemy the devil prowls around like a roaring lion looking for someone to devour. Resist him, standing firm in the faith" (1 Peter 5:8–9).

If you've ever seen a lion chase and devour a gazelle, you know we're not talking about Disney's *The Lion King*. No, the devil is a violent predator with bared teeth, eager to sink his teeth into his prey. This is how the devil chases after you and me! And I fear he's working harder to destroy us than we are to keep it from happening.

That's the bad news. The good news is that . . .

3. The Devil Responds to a Higher Authority

While the Bible describes demonic beings as "authorities" over certain worldly powers that they wield against us, their authority has a limit. Like defeated soldiers with no choice but to submit to an opposing officer, demons yield to God. They submit to his authority. They tremble at the name of Jesus. We're assured, "The one who is in you is greater than the one who is in the world" (1 John 4:4).

Three Spiritual Weapons

Now that you know these three spiritual realities, you also need to know the three weapons God provides to fight the enemy and his minions.

1. THE NAME OF JESUS

Without a doubt, the first weapon is the authority and power resident in the name of Jesus—it is the trump card over every demonic force. His name is the highest name in the heavenlies, and all of creation in every realm submits to it: "That at the name of Jesus every knee should bow, in heaven and on earth and under the earth" (Philippians 2:10).

During Christ's earthly ministry, his disciples were surprised to see the dramatic way demons responded when they used the name of Jesus. Upon hearing their report, Jesus described witnessing the moment when Satan fell:

> The seventy-two returned with joy and said, "Lord, even the demons submit to us in your name."
>
> He replied, "I saw Satan fall like lightning from heaven. I have given you authority to trample on snakes and scorpions and to overcome all the power of the enemy; nothing will harm you." (Luke 10:17–19)

As implied by comparing it to a flash of lightning, the "fight" between God and Lucifer didn't take very long. It wasn't a drawn-out war but merely a clash, flash, and crash showdown. Instead of a six-part Star Wars saga between the Force and the Dark Side, this heavenly battle was a one-scene surgical strike. I stress the difference to boost your confidence. So many people seem frightened by our enemy, as if spiritual warfare happens between two equal forces.

It does not.

2. THE BLOOD OF JESUS

Just as we can claim the power inherent in the name of Jesus, we can also claim the victory won by the blood of Jesus. The cross of Jesus Christ and his shed blood broke the curse of sin, the power of death, and the finality of the grave once and for all. Through his sacrificial death, Jesus atoned for our sins and paid the debt we could never pay. By accepting Christ, we overcome the enemy "by the blood of the Lamb" (Revelation 12:11).

How is that possible? Because sin is the source of the enemy's power. And Jesus paid for all sins forever. His blood was and is the ultimate defeat of the devil. Christ's blood has power to wash us white as snow, removing the ugly stain of sin. I'm reminded of these words from an old gospel hymn that celebrates this truth: "There is power, power, wonder-working power / In the precious blood of the Lamb."

3. THE WORD OF GOD

Our third weapon in battling the enemy is the Word of God. After fasting and praying in the desert for forty days, Jesus faced three distinct temptations from the devil. Each time, the Son of God responded by quoting Scripture, making his decision and his defense self-evident. God's Word instructs, informs, and inspires us, but it also protects us in spiritual warfare. When Paul urged us to "put on the full armor of God" in order to take our stand "against the devil's schemes," he correlated various parts of armor to aspects of our faith (Ephesians 6:11).

Our spiritual armor protects us from our enemy's attacks, but only the Word of God can serve as the sword of the Spirit (v. 17), an offensive weapon to dispel the devil's lies and pierce his temptations with the blade of truth.

Simply put, if you want to win your spiritual battles, you have to know your Bible. Reading God's Word not only draws you closer to him and reveals more of his character, it also provides a razor-sharp weapon against the enemy. I cannot encourage you enough to read your Bible and memorize verses and passages.

Start by finding a verse you can meditate on and pray for every struggle or problem. I've practiced this habit throughout most of my Christian life, and it never fails to bring me wisdom, insight, comfort, and peace. I like to have a verse for every situation, and while I encourage you to compile your own, this will get you started.

Verses to Pray When Facing Problems

Challenges
You, dear children, are from God and have overcome them, because the one who is in you is greater than the one who is in the world. (1 John 4:4)

Provision
My God will meet all your needs according to the riches of his glory in Christ Jesus. (Philippians 4:19)

Fear
The Lord is my light and my salvation—whom shall I fear? The Lord is the stronghold of my life—of whom shall I be afraid? (Psalm 27:1)

Sickness

Praise the Lord, my soul, and forget not all
his benefits—who forgives all your sins and
heals all your diseases. (Psalm 103:2–3)

Insecurity

He has made us competent as ministers of a new
covenant—not of the letter but of the Spirit; for the letter
kills, but the Spirit gives life. (2 Corinthians 3:6)

Danger

The Lord will watch over your coming and going
both now and forevermore. (Psalm 121:8).

Three Spiritual Practices

Now that you know three aspects of spiritual warfare and have three spiritual weapons in your arsenal, let's consider three daily practices to keep you in peak fighting condition. As you prepare, don't give in to fear; instead, rely on what you've been given. You already have the authority and power of God you need to win your battles.

When he was on earth, Jesus gave his disciples "authority to drive out impure spirits and to heal every disease and sickness" (Matthew 10:1). That same power is available to you and me. When we accept the free gift of salvation through Christ, the Holy Spirit dwells within us. We're literally empowered by God in us! And the Bible makes it clear that nothing can ever separate us from his love:

No, in all these things we are more than conquerors through him who loved us. For I am convinced that neither death nor life, neither angels nor demons, neither the present nor the future, nor any powers, neither height nor depth, nor anything else in all creation, will be able to separate us from the love of God that is in Christ Jesus our Lord. (Romans 8:37–39)

How can you put this spiritual power in you to work? Here are three spiritual practices you can use to give your faith a workout every day.

1. Daily Submit Yourself to God

While full access to Christ's authority is available, your authority against the devil is only as strong as your relationship with God. Here's the key: "Submit yourselves, then, to God. Resist the devil, and he will flee from you" (James 4:7–8).

Notice the order here. First, submit yourselves to God. Then, resist the devil and he will flee. It's like recharging our spiritual battery. It's your relationship with God that gives you power and authority. I don't rely on the name of Chris but the name of Christ! Which means I daily surrender myself to him as I walk by faith in the power of the Holy Spirit.

2. Close Any Open Doors That Give the Enemy Access

When you leave doors unlocked and wide open, it's an open invitation for someone to rob you. Thieves don't have to break in because you've given them a viable entrance and laid out the welcome mat.

The same principle applies with the enemy. When we disobey God, ignore his commandments, and yield to temptation, we give Satan a wide-open door to our lives. And one wide-open door we often overlook is unforgiveness. Forgiving others and seeking forgiveness is essential to our spiritual security system. The apostle Paul wrote to the church at Corinth, "Anyone you forgive, I also forgive. And what I have forgiven—if there was anything to forgive—I have forgiven in the sight of Christ for your sake, in order that Satan might not outwit us. For we are not unaware of his schemes" (2 Corinthians 2:10–11).

Paul warned us that when we fail to forgive, we create an opening for the devil to enter with his schemes. In fact, we can be outmaneuvered in a variety of ways, many of them revolving around an emotion that gets the best of us. Paul also warned, "In your anger do not sin: Do not let the sun go down while you are still angry, and do not give the devil a foothold" (Ephesians 4:26–27).

A strong spiritual defense requires closing all doors that you might open, whether intentionally or unintentionally. While you might wonder why anyone would intentionally invite the devil into their lives, that's often exactly what people do, sometimes even in the name of "innocent fun." For example, I refuse to participate in Halloween and cultural customs around it because God's Word warns us, "Have nothing to do with the fruitless deeds of darkness, but rather expose them" (Ephesians 5:11). If I'm overreacting, then the worst that can happen is I missed out on a lot of candy over the years. But if I'm trusting what the Bible says is true—and it is—then I can't be too cautious.

Wouldn't you rather err on the side of caution when dealing with the devil? Then I urge you to think carefully about associating with any works of darkness. Because you don't dwell in darkness once you've accepted Christ into your heart. He paid for your sins on the cross—past, present, and future. Your home in heaven is secure, but life here on earth can sometimes feel like hell. Don't let the devil find a crack in your defenses and wedge himself into your life.

Which brings us to the third practice for divine defense against darkness.

3. Confront the Enemy Every Day

Christianity is not passive. Prayer is both communion with God and confrontation with the devil. Living out your faith is about sharing God's truth and exposing the enemy's lies. We know, "When he lies, he speaks his native language, for he is a liar and the father of lies" (John 8:44). And a lie believed as truth will affect your life as if it were true.

So how do we proactively confront the devil?

Simple. We live in the fortress of God's truth, which liberates us from the evil one's lies. "Then you will know the truth, and the truth will set you free" (John 8:32). Knowing and living in truth, we can filter what we allow into our lives, our minds, and our hearts:

> For though we live in the world, we do not wage war as the world does. The weapons we fight with are not the weapons of the world. On the contrary, they have divine power to demolish strongholds. We demolish arguments and every pretension that sets itself up against the knowledge of God, and we take captive every thought to make it obedient to Christ. (2 Corinthians 10:3–5)

You may recall that the Greek word translated *strongholds* is *ochyroma* (okh-oo'-ro-mah), which refers to a prisoner locked up by deception. When we are trapped in a stronghold, we are living life based on something that's not true. But our knowledge of God and obedience to Christ enables us to "violently cast down" such strongholds. "Violently cast down" is the meaning of the Greek word *kathaireo* (kath-ahee-reh'-o), translated here as *demolish*. We have the authority and power to cast out dark angels—if we're willing to engage in warfare.

Our depression may not be caused by the devil alone, but he sure likes to use it as a wrecking ball in our lives if we let him. When we're depressed and anxious, we're vulnerable and typically more focused on our immediate pain than our eternal purpose. We allow emotions to overwhelm us and eclipse our thinking, which in turn can adversely impact our decisions and actions.

Many people have told me that depression leaves them feeling powerless. But I always try to remind them that despite how they may feel, they have access to the power of the living God right within them! Our battle belongs to him and doesn't rely on our own abilities. Our authority comes from his Word and from the name of his beloved Son, whose blood washed away our sins.

To aid you in spiritual warfare, I've included several prayers in the Resources section at the end of this book. Whether or not you pray these prayers or your own, it's important to be armed by God's Word at all times. You have spiritual power to demolish strongholds— including depression.

You only have to use it.

PART 3

Stepping into Solutions

CHAPTER 10

Stepping into a Needed Recovery

Come to me, all of you who are weary and
carry heavy burdens, and I will give you rest.
—JESUS, MATTHEW 11:28 NLT

Most of us know we can't neglect ourselves and expect to stay grounded, let alone make up for the stress, exhaustion, and busyness that have become the plague of twenty-first-century life. As we've seen, such a frantic lifestyle leaves us vulnerable to depression, anxiety, and spiritual attack. We still live that way, though, don't we? Or maybe I should just speak for myself.

But I suspect most of us have been pushed to our limits at some point. Looking back, I know I've never been more exhausted than I was the year that COVID-19 turned the world upside down. It didn't help matters that I was already depleted and in need of a break when the pandemic first took hold.

I had started 2020 with twenty-one days of prayer and fasting, a period of drawing close to God and seeking his will. This is a practice we've done together as a church community for many years. By the end of January, I was off and running, my schedule filled with all the items I'd put on hold during my twenty-one days. In February, our church continued growing as we started new campuses in additional locations. My travel schedule also picked up, culminating in a trip to Israel at the beginning of March with my friend and mentor John Maxwell.

Just as countries were closing borders and quarantining visitors, John and I managed to catch the last flight from Tel Aviv back to the States. When I arrived in Birmingham, I immediately had to make dozens of decisions about how Highlands would respond to COVID-19—everything from reviewing the message to send out to our members, to planning online services, to jumping in with ways to serve our community. In the weeks that followed, our team, like thousands of others in our country, scrambled to figure out how to do church online, including Easter services.

By the time what should have been spring break rolled around in April, I was at my breaking point. Tired all the time and irritable from the relentless pace I'd been keeping, I wasn't thinking clearly. I had neglected my body's need for rest and recovery—but just as important, I had ignored the diminishing health of my soul. I'm more than old enough to know better, but there I was at the end of my rope once again, asking God to catch me.

Rather than take a weekend off or delegate more, I knew I needed to focus on replenishing my physical, mental, emotional, and spiritual health. I had been dismissing the importance of self-care—after all, I'm a tough guy, a strong leader, a dedicated pastor, empowered by the Spirit of the living God. But the Holy Spirit made it clear that I was not being a good steward.

I've been quick to preach balance, rest, and soul care to thousands of people around the world, but slower to implement it in my own life. I realized that I had to *do* soul care, not just talk about it. After all, it was not my idea but God's. After he created the world and everything in it and declared it good, he rested on the seventh day. Obviously, the all-powerful and eternal God does not need physical rest as you and I need rest, but the Lord still considered resting on the seventh day important enough that he set an example for us. Not to mention that he also included rest in the Ten Commandments: "Remember to observe the Sabbath day . . . the seventh day is a day of rest dedicated to the LORD your God (Exodus 20:8, 10 NLT). We can also follow the example of Jesus, who often stepped out of ministry demands to enjoy time alone with his Father, and who provided times of rest for his disciples: "Come with me by yourselves to a quiet place and get some rest" (Mark 6:31).

So I went away to rest for eight days—with no phone, no urgent texts and e-mails, no decisions. It was heaven on earth! I was reminded that the body and mind can only take so much. Going away to rest, recover, and renew may sound self-indulgent, but it is essential if we want to be the best stewards of the primary resources God has entrusted to us—our body, soul, and spirit.

When I was younger, I had to learn this lesson the hard way. And while I still drag my feet and often wait longer than I should to take the rest I need, I know when I'm near my limits and need to get away. I've learned it's hard to pour anything out of an empty cup.

If you want to win against depression, you have to let God fill you again.

And that means taking care of the vessel he's given you.

When the Journey Is Too Much

Elijah may not have faced the same pressures we face, but this doesn't mean his depletion and depression were any less intense. Based on the details in his story, I can't help but wonder if he, too, had neglected caring for his body, soul, and spirit. Because one of the most striking parts of Elijah's journey through depression to health and freedom is his encounter with God's angel.

Considering Elijah's circumstances and role as God's chosen prophet, we might expect the angel came to deliver a purely spiritual message. Something like, "You're a man of God—act like it!" Or, "God is with you—be bold in his power!" Or even, "You're a prophet and miracle worker—just have faith!" Instead, the angel focused on Elijah's physical needs:

> Then [Elijah] lay down under the bush and fell asleep. All at once an angel touched him and said, "Get up and eat." He looked around, and there by his head was some bread baked over hot coals, and a jar of water. He ate and drank and then lay down again.
>
> The angel of the LORD came back a second time and touched him and said, "Get up and eat, for the journey is too much for you." So he got up and ate and drank. Strengthened by that food, he traveled forty days and forty nights until he reached Horeb, the mountain of God. (1 Kings 19:5–8)

Perhaps our physical needs are more important than we realize, especially when we're wandering in the fog of depression. Our body's requirements may even be more spiritual than we think. Elijah needed sleep. And then food and water. And more sleep. And more food. Maybe when our bodies and minds receive the rest and nourishment they need, we're then receptive to God working in us.

Elijah's cycles of sleep and nourishment seem like Self-Care 101. This isn't self-indulgence in luxury accommodations—it's what we learned as children and what many of us taught our own little ones: rest when you're tired, sleep when you're sleepy, eat when you're hungry, drink when you're thirsty. If we care for toddlers or even older children, we make sure they drink enough water, eat nutritious food, and get enough sleep.

Yet, I'm guessing you may have disregarded these same basic principles of self-care and experienced the same crash I've endured after running too long on adrenaline, caffeine, sugar, and carbs. As adults who supposedly know better, we repeatedly push ourselves beyond our limits and then wonder what's wrong with us. That was a significant factor in my major panic attack in Australia—I had ignored what I knew my body needed. And I know so many people who work and serve and volunteer and travel and work some more and then seem shocked when they collapse. Sometimes they're just dehydrated and sleep deprived. Other times it's more serious because exceeding their limits has caused greater damage to their bodies, minds, and spirits.

So take note: God's first remedy for Elijah's depression was physical rest and nourishment. Sleep and food are both gifts from God. The psalmist described the natural blessings God bestows on us: "He makes grass grow for the cattle, and plants for people to cultivate—bringing forth food from the earth: wine that gladdens human hearts, oil to make their faces shine, and bread that sustains their hearts" (Psalm 104:14–15).

Just as food nourishes the body, a good night's sleep, one not interrupted by insomnia or bad dreams, does wonders for our emotional state. The psalmist wrote, "In vain you rise early and stay up late, toiling for food to eat—for he grants sleep to those he loves" (Psalm 127:2). When your body feels rested, it increases the odds that your mind will be rested as well. When you're physically fatigued, mentally drained, and emotionally exhausted, you've set yourself up for depression. Everything in you is signaling, "Red alert!"

I love how God dealt with Elijah so tenderly and kindly, particularly in light of the distance the prophet had covered. Elijah ran 17 miles ahead of Ahab to Jezreel, and then from Mount Carmel to

Beersheba, about another 120 miles. On foot, this distance would take a traveler around six days unless he ran most of the way. Elijah also spent a day running into the wilderness before following the Lord's instruction to go all the way to Mount Horeb. According to pastor and scholar Tony Merida, "That all adds up to about 300 miles! When we're physically tired, we're spiritually vulnerable as well."[1]

Elijah had just traveled many miles, likely over several months, running away from an empty threat made by a bitter idolater who had lost face in the sacrifice showdown. Yet, God didn't come to scold Elijah, "You coward! What are you doing under a bush in the desert? Get up and shake it off!"

No, God provided for Elijah's most immediate and basic needs. He didn't put him down. He didn't criticize him. He didn't condemn him. He didn't even challenge him to dig deeper or persevere. What he did was send an angel to encourage this depleted human being to take some food and rest. Restoring Elijah's health was God's starting point.

Too often, I suspect, we struggle to be this kind to ourselves. It seems easier to berate ourselves or to give up: "What's wrong with me? I'm such a loser!" "Nothing matters. Take me, Lord. I give up." Instead of berating yourself, what if you treated yourself as God treated Elijah? How might things be different if you went to bed at a regular time and consistently got enough sleep? Drank enough water? Were intentional about eating food that's actually good for you? Those are the basics.

From there, maybe treating yourself with kindness in the midst of your depression is simply going for a walk. Or getting up on time in the morning so you can shower, groom, and dress before eating a breakfast that will fuel your body. Maybe it's going to the gym and not following a routine but just doing something you love—swimming, stretching, Zumba, soaking in the hot tub, or sweating in the sauna.

Before God addressed Elijah's spiritual needs, he attended to Elijah's physical needs. And strengthened by food and rest, the prophet continued on his journey. So, if you're battling depression, first things first. It's time to do what you can to meet your body's basic physical and emotional needs.

Physical Needs

Let's first consider what may be missing in your life. If you are going to receive the same help that God gave Elijah, it's important to assess your lifestyle and the toll it's taking on you physically and mentally. You may already know some changes need to be made in order to practice basic self-care. But if you're serious about overcoming depression, then it's time to face some facts.

The following assessment includes several continuums to help you better understand where you are right now in six categories: diet, sleep, relationships, hobbies, exercise, and rest/reflection. Each continuum uses a one-to-ten scale. Circle the number on the continuum that best describes your response.

DIET

1   2   3   4   5   6   7   8   9   10

My eating habits consistently diminish my health.   My eating habits consistently enhance my health.

1   2   3   4   5   6   7   8   9   10

I never drink water throughout the day.   I always drink water throughout the day.

SLEEP

1　　2　　3　　4　　5　　6　　7　　8　　9　　10

I never get enough
sleep each night to
feel rested.

I always get enough
sleep each night to
feel rested.

RELATIONSHIPS

1　　2　　3　　4　　5　　6　　7　　8　　9　　10

I never connect
in life-giving
relationships
with others.

I always connect
in life-giving
relationships
with others.

HOBBIES

1　　2　　3　　4　　5　　6　　7　　8　　9　　10

I never engage
in activities that
rejuvenate me.

I always engage
in activities that
rejuvenate me.

EXERCISE

1　　2　　3　　4　　5　　6　　7　　8　　9　　10

I never engage
in exercise or
activities to keep
my body healthy.

I always engage
in exercise or
activities to keep
my body healthy.

REST AND REFLECTION

1　　2　　3　　4　　5　　6　　7　　8　　9　　10

I never make time
for rest and reflection.

I always make time
for rest and reflection.

Briefly review your responses. What stands out most to you? Which categories are taking the greatest toll on your health? If your body could speak, what might it say to you?

So often when we're overwhelmed by depression, feeling either sad and hopeless or numb and withdrawn, we believe we're powerless. As we've seen in previous chapters, when we feel powerless to make our depression go away, we do nothing. But doctors and psychologists are finding that even the smallest changes can help us feel empowered and remind us that we have options and choices.

Elijah needed sleep and nourishment before he could continue on his journey. We need the same things. Before we can continue on our path of healing and restoration, we need to be strengthened by sleep and nourishment. Once those needs have been met, we're ready to resume our journey to God's next divine destination.

Emotional Needs

We not only need to tend to our physical needs, but also to our emotional needs. I like to use a construction metaphor when looking at emotional health because it allows us to consider different emotional components and functions. Just as quality building materials produce a solid, stable structure, healthy emotions produce a solid structure for living.

A balanced emotional foundation includes everything from the ability to handle adversity, failure, and criticism, to navigating change and pressure without causing structural damage to your emotional house. We all go through hard times and disappointments as well as triumphs and celebrations. For some people, the downturns can lead to anxiety and depression, yet others quickly bounce back when facing similar adversities. What explains the difference?

Although the answer to this question can be complex, I believe one of the key reasons is that well-balanced and resilient people have done the work required to build a strong emotional foundation before the crisis hit. The storms of life will always come, sooner or later, and often without warning. And when they do, they will reveal our foundation for what it really is.

Crisis has a way of amplifying weaknesses and dispensing with façades. When we face a season of strife, stress, and struggle, we find out who we really are. Intense pressure and stress can bring out the best in people, but it can also bring out the worst. We can be generous and compassionate one moment, and then become enraged at the slightest offense the next.

Crisis inevitably reveals our emotional capacity and strength of character. For example, if we look at key moments in the lives of Jesus' disciples, we catch glimpses of their emotional strengths and weaknesses when under duress. Like many of us, they often let their emotions get the best of them when faced with unexpected danger.

When they were in a boat with Jesus and a storm blew up, the disciples were overwhelmed by fear and anxiety (Mark 4:36–38). No matter how much they wanted to trust Jesus, and no matter how much what they knew about his power and astounding miracles, their immediate crisis caused them to hit the panic button. Lurching waves, harsh winds, and pounding rain short-circuited their faith, even when the Son of God himself was with them in the boat.

To be honest, I don't blame them one bit. We all tend to think the worst during times of crisis and uncertainty. I consider myself an emotionally stable person, but I've still been blindsided by circumstances that left me reeling. Which is exactly why practicing habits that strengthen the foundation of our emotional house is so important. If our foundation is solid, our emotional and spiritual structures will stand strong even when the storms of life hit hard.

You may recall that Jesus used the metaphor of building a house to describe how we practice our faith in the face of adversity:

> Everyone who hears these words of mine and puts them into practice is like a *wise man* who *built his house* on the rock. The rain came

down, the streams rose, and the winds blew and beat against that house; yet *it did not fall*, because it had its *foundation* on the rock. (Matthew 7:24–25, emphasis added)

When faith in Christ is our bedrock foundation, we're ready when life's storms hit. They may blow us around, leave us soaked, and rip a few shingles off the roof. But our house stands strong!

How we build the foundation of our emotional house is vitally important. If we focus on the quality of our relationship with God and establish habits that prepare, protect, and provide during storms, we won't fear being destroyed by worst-case scenarios and devastating losses. They will still hurt and knock us down sometimes, but they don't destroy us. Why? Because our house is built on the Rock of Ages.

When you build a house, you focus first on the big structural elements and then work your way down to smaller details. Every house needs a foundation, walls, and a roof. It needs structural supports to hold up the interior framework of floors, ceilings, beams, and rafters. Then decorative elements add beauty, style, and personality to the overall interior design, usually in harmony with the exterior.

With these parts in mind, let's consider how we can either renovate or rebuild our emotional houses with faith-based materials. And before we unpack these, I must credit my friend Dr. Henry Cloud, a clinical psychologist and bestselling Christian author. Much of what I'm about to share with you has been adapted from what I've learned from him about emotional health and its relationship to spiritual maturity.

How Firm a Foundation

Most homebuilders begin by pouring a concrete foundation. Even if they use other materials, such as stone, brick, or wood, no builder would think of building a house with only the barren ground as a foundation. I suppose the emotional and spiritual parallel would be trying to live your life without the foundation of a belief system—just drifting with your moods, cultural influences, and the agendas of others. No one wants to live passively dependent this way when you have been given free will, intelligence, and resources to live with purpose and meaning.

To secure our emotional foundations, we need strong relationships and connectedness. The foundation of every human being is their relational connectedness. Connectedness—with loved ones, friends, neighbors, colleagues, coworkers, peers—grounds us. We need each other and are only as healthy as our relationships. Each of us has an important part to play as we rely on one another in order to function as one body: "From him the whole body, joined and held together by every supporting ligament, grows and builds itself up in love, as each part does its work" (Ephesians 4:16).

To maintain emotional stability, it's essential to cultivate healthy relationships with people who pour life back into you. You need individuals as well as groups who inspire you, challenge you, encourage you, and help you be more of who God made you to be. Making sure you're getting the emotional nourishment you need also means eliminating or minimizing toxic, unhealthy relationships with people who hurt you, weaken you, undermine you, or tempt you to disobey God.

Remember, your relationships—with God and others—determine how your foundation weathers life's storms.

Structural Support

Balanced emotional support and stability also comes from your life's structures. The frame of your house should support your purpose. Instead of beams, studs, and rafters, your emotional structure relies on habits, practices, and routines. Your purpose defines how you live your life, and your habits and practices help you live it out.

When you develop schedules and maintain routines, your brain relaxes. Your mind sees that you have allocated time, energy, and necessary resources to accomplish goals, fulfill commitments, and practice habits—all related to living out your life's purpose. If you can't see how something you're doing regularly relates to who God has called you to be, then it's time to reconsider that activity or practice. You may need to replace it with something that connects more directly to your God-given purpose.

On the other hand, when you don't have some way of bringing order to the daily chaos of life, your mind and body remain on red alert. Then you're in perpetual fight-flight-freeze mode, unsure of what to do next and for how long. You lose sight of priorities because whatever feels urgent commands your energy and attention.

This explains why the COVID-19 pandemic unsettled nearly everyone. Suddenly, we were stripped of our usual way of doing things and forced to abandon productive routines and familiar habits. Working from home or going to school through distance learning, we had to find new ways of restoring order and scheduling our days. We improvised and adjusted in order to take shelter from the storms all around us.

What constants keep us centered as we adapt—or any time life tries to overwhelm us? *Remembering our purpose and structuring our habits and practices around it.*

When we remind ourselves of our purpose, we realize what's most important hasn't changed. Our health, finances, and lifestyle may have changed, but our God-given calling has not. So when life's storms leave you feeling battered and bruised, go back to that moment when you discovered why you were put on this earth. If you're still in the process of discovering why God made you the way he did and what he wants you to do, then focus on what you already know. We're not just existing during our time on earth; each of us is on a mission for our Maker. We each have a purpose that's bigger than ourselves as we pursue the work God has for us, a mission that matters for eternity.

In a world filled with uncertainty and unknowns, we must focus on God's vision for our lives. Keeping his vision front and center brings stability, confidence, and clarity even when everything around us feels like shifting sand. The Bible says, "Where there is no vision, the people perish" (Proverbs 29:18 KJV). Here's another translation that provides a unique insight into this verse: "Where there is no *revelation*, people cast off *restraint*" (Proverbs 29:18, emphasis added). In other words, if you don't have a clear vision for your life, you'll think it doesn't matter how you live. But it does matter.

Right now, you may need a reminder that God has a specific and amazing plan for your life—and that following his plan is the only thing that will bring you real fulfillment. With God's vision supporting your emotional structure, you gain clarity about your priorities.

Getting your priorities in order allows you to take control of your schedule and your habits. Start by developing a morning routine that sets you up for enjoying the most successful day possible. I'm a firm believer that "all's well that begins well." Nearly everyone has more peace when they have a clear schedule in place. You have a sense of what's ahead and can prepare accordingly. Even when events change and derail your schedule, your preparations still matter. You take control of the decisions that you can—such as how to respond to a cancelled appointment—and let go of the ones you can't.

Experiment with your schedule and routines and find what works best for you. To give you a starting point, I'll share how I arrange my days to stay focused. A few years ago, I received a Full Focus Planner from my friend Michael Hyatt. Impressed by its emphasis on divine purpose, I made it a part of my quiet time each morning. It helps me take a few minutes to focus in on the three tasks that I want to prioritize that day. If those three get done, I'm happy to hit my target. If they don't, I'm reminded to add or adjust them the following day.

If you want to build a strong, steady structure for your emotional house, let your calling determine your commitments and schedule accordingly.

Interior Design

Once your foundation and support structures are in place, it's time to decorate the rooms. While you might use paint, wallpaper, and architectural details to stylize the interior of a house, you beautify your emotional house with attributes such as trust, wisdom, and self-control. The most beautiful lives I've seen are those that reflect complete trust in God. These people only try to control what they can control—and leave the rest to the Lord.

That may be the essence of wisdom in a nutshell, understanding the difference between a fact of life and a problem. Facts of life are matters you cannot always, if ever, control. Problems, on the other hand, can usually be fixed. To live in peace and harmony, it's important to learn to discern the difference and live accordingly. As you grow in experience and practice, you develop wisdom.

The key to growing in wisdom is trusting God enough to give up control of what you cannot control. You may feel angry, frustrated, disappointed, anxious, and afraid, but if you can't control whatever's causing those feelings, then it's time to trust God to handle it. When struggling in these situations, my friend Henry Cloud recommends making a list of everything bothering you that you can't control. Get a pad of paper and a pen (or your laptop), set a timer for ten minutes, and then worry all you want on the page: bad weather, your boss's mood at the board meeting, your child's broken arm, the stock market's impact on your retirement—on and on.

When the timer goes off, discard your list. Crumple the page and toss it in the bin or hit the delete key. Give it to God and let go of every item you wrote down, as well as the ones you didn't!

Another practice that helps when you feel distressed is prayer. When life feels out of control, I've found great comfort and peace from praying theologian Reinhold Niebuhr's beautiful prayer, popularly known as the Serenity Prayer.[2]

> God, grant me the serenity to accept the things I cannot change, the courage to change the things I can, and the wisdom to know the difference. Living one day at a time, enjoying one moment at a time; accepting hardship as a pathway to peace; taking, as Jesus did, this sinful world as it is, not as I would have it; trusting that you will make all things right if I surrender to your will; so that I may be reasonably happy in this life and supremely happy with you forever in the next. Amen.

This prayer addresses our needs for both divine trust and self-control. Trust is giving up control of what you can't control—and the best way is to pray. And self-control is the opposite: doing what you can to control the things you can control. The Serenity Prayer reminds us to seek wisdom to know the difference because either extreme—trust or self-control—won't work alone. We must practice both.

As we trust, we also need to practice self-control. Think of this as exercising wisdom and faith at the same time. Self-control is simply taking responsibility for whatever is within my power to control. Remember what Dr. George Crane said: "Motions are the precursors of emotions." Even when we can't control how we feel, we can control our choices and actions in the midst of our emotions. We exercise the options that we know are good for us and avoid the ones that pull us deeper into our caves.

You have options about how you care for your body, soul, and spirit. It's all about making daily decisions.

You may affirm that these principles are true, but they won't change your life until you act on them. Commit to spending time with God each day. Arrange your schedule and your habits to reflect his vision for your life as you live out your purpose. When the storms come, and they always do in this life, your house will stand strong.

CHAPTER 11

Stepping into a God Encounter

Faith means trusting in advance what
will only make sense in reverse.
—Philip Yancey

This is your captain speaking—please make sure your seatbelts are securely fastened. We're going to be experiencing some rough air, and it could be very bumpy at times."

Oh, great, I thought. *What a day to be flying!*

Looking out my little cubbyhole window, I could see massive clouds bruising the sky in shades of gray, dark blue, and inky violet. The dreary darkness made it seem like nightfall instead of the middle of the day. Rain splattered against the plane, its patter reminding me of drops falling on a tin roof. Only I wasn't holed up in a cozy cabin where I could nap to its soothing rhythm. No, I was about to go right up into the belly of those clouds and into the eye of the storm.

Gusts of wind shook the plane as we waited our turn on the runway. I'm a seasoned flyer, and I've been through some in-flight turbulence before, but this entire day left me with a bad feeling.

Too late now, I thought, as we finally began to speed down the runway. I closed my eyes to pray and entrust our ascent to God. The wings of the plane caught drafts and wobbled back and forth as we forcefully gained altitude and pushed through the sky.

Higher and higher we climbed until suddenly sunlight washed over us. Breaking through the sky's lid of storm clouds, the plane now hovered above them. Brilliant blue skies stretched over the dark, tufted carpet below as the sun smiled back at me with its dazzling white-gold rays. I felt like an astronaut who had just discovered another world! Such beauty and tranquility coexisting right above the dismal, dark scene below the cloud line.

The whole scene struck me as a vivid illustration of two realities always present in our lives. There's the reality we live at ground level, where we're battered by storms beyond our control. Then there's the reality we live at God's level, looking down on our storms from above where the sun is always shining. That bright view is there all the time, though we don't always take notice of it. And yet, it's this heavenly perspective that can change how we see things here on the ground.

Let It Out

Without a doubt, a change in perspective can transform your view of everything. When Jesus was teaching about the end times to his disciples, he shared a glimpse of the chaos and destruction we would experience on earth. But he stressed that these events, as terrible and painful as they would be, would also signal the culmination of our salvation: "When these things begin to take place, stand up and lift up your heads, because your redemption is drawing near" (Luke 21:28).

In other words, we should look up, not around.

When we're looking for purpose and hope in life, we have to get beyond the external fog and internal smog. We have to see through the smokescreens, both within and without, and seek God's perspective.

We have to remember our true position—that we are seated with Christ in the heavenly places (Ephesians 2:6). Even though we haven't yet taken our place there for eternity, that is the perspective from which we need to view everything we face on the ground. With all the challenges most of us are navigating, limiting our view to an earthly perspective will only stress us out and bring us down.

That's the trap Elijah fell into—he lost his ability to see clearly because he kept looking around at his circumstances rather than up to God. He needed God's perspective, and the Lord gave it to him. But not before attending to Elijah's needs for rest and nourishment. Once God's prophet was physically refreshed, he received instructions to travel to Mount Horeb, also known as Mount Sinai. That's where God had previously revealed himself to Moses, so it makes sense that God would also summon Elijah there for a divine appointment.

Elijah traveled forty days and nights to reach Mount Horeb. In Scripture, forty is often the number of preparation, and it often signifies time set aside for prayer and fasting.[1] Once Elijah's body had recovered from the long journey, he was soon ready for the next step. Based on his example, we can surmise that getting physically healthy alone is not the end of the journey to overcoming depression—it's only the beginning. The ultimate help comes from an encounter with God.

Once Elijah arrived on the mountain, his depression resurfaced:

> There he went into a cave and spent the night. And the word of the LORD came to him: "What are you doing here, Elijah?"
>
> He replied, "I have been very zealous for the LORD God Almighty. The Israelites have rejected your covenant, torn down your altars, and put your prophets to death with the sword. I am the only one left, and now they are trying to kill me too." (1 Kings 19:9–10)

Notice the curious details in this exchange. First, it began with Elijah arriving and going into a cave to spend the night. Maybe he was afraid of lions or wolves and didn't want to camp out in the open, but symbolically he retreated into darkness. Then God asked him what he was doing there. Now, God clearly knew what Elijah was doing there—the prophet had been led there to meet the Lord! And even though God knew the answer without asking, he wanted Elijah to express his feelings.

God actually likes for us to do that—share all that we're feeling without holding back. God wasn't shocked or disappointed by Elijah, and he's not surprised when we vent and unload our worries. God made us and knows that it's unhealthy to keep our feelings inside. It's when we aren't in touch with them or willing to share them with God and others that our emotions contribute to our depression.

In 1 Kings 19, the passage conveys six different emotions that Elijah experienced and then expressed in his ongoing conversations with the Lord:

- **Fear:** "Elijah was afraid" (v. 3).
- **Desperation:** "I have had enough" (v. 4).
- **Low self-esteem**: "I am no better than my ancestors" (v. 4).
- **Anger:** "I have been very zealous for the LORD God Almighty" (v. 10), which might be rephrased as, "I've worked hard for nothing."
- **Loneliness:** "I am the only one left" (v. 10).
- **Worry/anxiety:** "They're trying to kill me" (v. 10).

These six emotions are the basic recipe for depression! No wonder God wanted Elijah to air out his emotions. Any one of these can be overwhelming, but when they collide, they create an even more potent poison. Until Elijah expressed the emotions that were wearing him down, he wouldn't be able to move forward.

How about you?

What needs to be expressed to God?

What feelings have you pushed down inside and kept from God and others?

One-on-One Encounter

Elijah's honesty and desperation led him to an encounter with God. Perhaps expressing his feelings and letting go of them created space for Elijah to receive what God wanted to give him. Because after the prophet let off some steam, the Lord made it clear he had something he wanted Elijah to experience:

> The Lord said, "Go out and stand on the mountain in the presence of the Lord, for the Lord is about to pass by."
>
> Then a great and powerful wind tore the mountains apart and shattered the rocks before the Lord, but the Lord was not in the wind. After the wind there was an earthquake, but the Lord was not in the earthquake. After the earthquake came a fire, but the Lord was not in the fire. And after the fire came a gentle whisper. When Elijah heard it, he pulled his cloak over his face and went out and stood at the mouth of the cave.
>
> Then a voice said to him, "What are you doing here, Elijah?"
> (1 Kings 19:11–13)

Elijah stood there and God revealed his identity. Keep in mind that Elijah was already familiar with big, dynamic displays of God's power—he had prayed and watched God's holy fire consume not only a drenched sacrifice but also the stones of a wet altar and the trench of water around it. So in one sense, God began his encounter with Elijah with demonstrations of power that would have been familiar to the prophet, perhaps as if to say, "I'm still in control, still powerful, still the same God you've been serving."

But God also wanted to show himself to Elijah in a different way.

What really got Elijah's attention was the gentle whisper that came after the windstorm, earthquake, and fire. The fact of the matter is, God usually speaks to us in stillness and quietness. Not in some big dramatic demonstration of fire or power. God reminded Elijah that he was still right there beside him.

Most of us want God to do something spectacular to rescue us when we're suffering, but often he would rather whisper to us. In Scripture, God sometimes used big and dramatic displays to reveal himself to many people all at once, just as he had done when he sent fire from heaven to consume the sacrifice at Mount Carmel. Here, God did all that for Elijah more as a reminder; then he whispered and made it clear this was a one-on-One encounter.

At Mount Carmel, God showed up for everyone.
At Mount Horeb, God showed up for Elijah.
At Mount Carmel, God was spectacular for everyone.
At Mount Horeb, God was spectacular for Elijah.

Hearing the intimate whisper of God's voice spoken just for him, Elijah pulled his cloak over his face and went out and stood at the cave's entrance. His response symbolizes the awe that often follows when we encounter the living God in such a close and personal way. We want to reduce the focus on ourselves so we can take in more of God. We symbolically cloak our faces—not to hide from him, but out of reverence and respect. We long for more of him and want to live our lives to please him. At that point, we are no longer consumed by our emotions.

Elijah also stepped forward to the threshold of a new beginning.

He stood there above the clouds with a new view on life and his future. When we encounter God, we also gain the confidence and ability to step forward and leave the darkness of our cave. Notice that Elijah wasn't yet fully out of the cave, but he stood at its mouth. Once again, this emphasizes the process of leaving depression behind in steps and stages. As we'll explore in the remaining chapters, Elijah had more steps to take—and so do we.

Embrace the Struggle

Although overcoming depression is indeed a process, there's no substitute for an intimate encounter with the power and presence of God. Knowing him personally is the greatest antidepressant available in our spiritual battle for health and wholeness. Rarely do we experience instant curative healing from our depression, but a fresh awareness of God's presence and perspective will almost always get us moving again.

I suspect our most powerful encounters with God occur in the midst of our darkest depressions. I'll never forget being a teenager and experiencing depression for the first time. It remains one of the three darkest seasons of my life and the only time I've ever considered suicide. I experienced a major disruption, disappointment, or division in every area of my life. I had girl trouble, friend trouble, and trouble with the law. My parents didn't understand, and I didn't know how to explain what was going on and how I felt. My grades and activities at school suffered. Then I had an encounter with God that changed the direction of my entire life.

When we're having our darkest moments, God moves in our lives because we have nowhere left to turn. He's always present with us, even in our worst times, but we have to look for him and listen for his whisper. God's Word promises, "The LORD is close to the brokenhearted and saves those who are crushed in spirit" (Psalm 34:18). When we're at our lowest, God has our full attention because we've usually exhausted our own attempts to solve problems and numb our emotions. When life is going great and we're feeling self-sufficient, we may give him credit but not our undivided attention.

God meets us where we are—always.

But our response to him determines what happens next.

I know what you're thinking. *You make it sound so easy, Chris. I would love for God to show up right now—I need a deep encounter! But I can't make it happen. It feels like such a struggle to even pray. Or do anything!*

I get it. Sometimes when we feel like we need God most, we feel too far away to find him. We're consumed by the struggles of each day, preoccupied with the devastating sadness in our lives. We want to surrender to him and experience his arms around us, but something in us resists him too.

Wrestling with our thoughts, our feelings and doubts, our pain, we feel like some invisible force prevents us from taking a step toward God. We want to get up and go to the mouth of our cave, but we can't. There's just no energy. No hope.

I understand—I really do. But in these wrestling matches with our emotions, we must embrace the struggle. We have to muster whatever faith we can and push through, even when we don't think we can. Perhaps especially when we don't feel like it.

WrestleMania

When I think of wrestling, I always consider Jacob in the Old Testament. Arguably, he knew the struggle of wrestling—with himself, with others, with God—better than anyone. Jacob was the grandson of Abraham and the son of Isaac.

After deceiving and making a mortal enemy of Esau, his twin brother, Jacob went on the run. He eventually settled with relatives and started over, though more family drama ensued as he married two sisters. After a decades in exile, enough was enough and Jacob longed to return home, but he knew he'd have to face his past. Here's what happened the night before Jacob met Esau again, not knowing if Esau would accept him or kill him.

That night Jacob got up and took his two wives, his two female servants and his eleven sons and crossed the ford of the Jabbok. After he had sent them across the stream, he sent over all his possessions. So Jacob was left alone, and *a man wrestled with him till daybreak.* When the man saw that he could not overpower him, he touched the socket of Jacob's hip so that his hip was wrenched as he *wrestled* with the man. Then the man said, "Let me go, for it is daybreak."

But Jacob replied, "I will not let you go unless you bless me."

The man asked him, "What is your name?"

"Jacob," he answered.

Then the man said, "Your name will no longer be Jacob, but Israel, because you have *struggled with God* and with humans and have overcome."

Jacob said, "Please tell me your name."

But he replied, "Why do you ask my name?" Then he blessed him there.

So Jacob called the place Peniel, saying, "It is because I saw God *face to face*, and yet my life was spared." (Genesis 32:22–30, emphasis added)

I love this scene so much because it merges Jacob's physical wrestling with his emotional wrestling. He was simultaneously wrestling with his past, with his secrets, and with his God.

To enhance our understanding, let's think about the way wrestling works both physically and emotionally. In the sport of wrestling, two opponents try to overpower each other through specific holds, moves, lifts, throws, and pins. In today's world of wrestling entertainment, the whole process includes exaggerated actions as well as sensational characters and narratives. In the sport of internal wrestling—which we do spiritually, emotionally, and psychologically—we feel pulled in opposing directions by our mistakes and our goals, by our past and our future, by who we think we are and who God thinks we are. The pain, chaos, and tendency to exaggerate may be just as intense as anything we might witness on WrestleMania.

Jacob was forced to wrestle with everything he had worked for decades to avoid, to deny, to escape. But as he led his family to his homeland, he finally realized that he could no longer run away from who he had been and what he had done. He knew it was time to face his past. He had to take responsibility for his lying, cheating, and deceiving.

Like Jacob, we often find ourselves in a wrestling match between who we've become and who we're supposed to be. Often when we're at our lowest and most desperate, we reach a point where we know we have to change. And in order to take steps forward and leave our cave behind, we're going to have to embrace the struggle. It's a struggle that requires us to wrestle with the same things Jacob faced: the past, our secrets and their consequences, and God.

Stop to Start

Whether you believe you've made choices better or worse than Jacob's, your past may be what's keeping you from moving out of your cave and closer to God. Most of us expend far too much energy thinking about how we got where we are and what we should have done differently. But the past is the past—you can't unscramble eggs, as the saying goes. It's done. No matter how hard you try or how desperately you try to compensate, you cannot change your past.

You can only start again from where you are right now, in this moment. And while you can't go back and change the beginning of your story, you can start where you are and change where you end up. The Bible tells us, "But if from there you seek the LORD your God, you will find him if you seek him with all your heart and with all your soul" (Deuteronomy 4:29). In other words, don't try to settle yesterday—start from today!

So how do you start from where you are? You must get rid of your rearview mirror. God's Word urges, "Forget the former things; do not dwell on the past. See, I am doing a new thing! Now it springs up; do you not perceive it? I am making a way in the wilderness and streams in the wasteland" (Isaiah 43:18–19).

It's time to move on—let the past be the past.

But to make a clean break, we must also wrestle with any secrets we've been keeping. We know who we are—who God has created and called us to be—but we hide behind a false front in order to maintain our secrets. But the more we cling to our secrets, the more power they have over us. Over time, we begin to take on the identity of our illness, shame, regret, guilt, and disappointment.

It's interesting to note that Jacob's initial deception was literally pretending to be someone else, his brother Esau (Genesis 27–28). That meant he only received his father's blessing by pretending to be someone he wasn't. Although his deception succeeded in getting him exactly what he wanted, he never got to enjoy it. It cost him his family, his peace, and decades in exile.

Like Jacob, we can pretend to be someone we're not in order to get what we think we want. But just as Jacob discovered, we get what we want only to be haunted by how we got it. Sometimes we work so much harder at hiding than at healing. God cannot bless who we pretend to be: "Whoever conceals their sins does not prosper, but the one who confesses and renounces them finds mercy" (Proverbs 28:13).

If we want a life-changing, depression-crushing encounter with God, we must come clean. We must take off our masks, own up to our secrets, and confess them before God and others. Otherwise, our secrets eat away at us. They make us sick, physically and emotionally, until we let go of them and embrace God's grace. The psalmist expressed this beautifully:

> When I *refused to confess* my sin,
>   my body wasted away,
>   and I groaned all day long.
> Day and night your hand of discipline was heavy on me.
>   My *strength evaporated* like water in the summer heat. . .
> Finally, *I confessed* all my sins to you
>   and *stopped trying to hide* my guilt.
> I said to myself, "I will confess my rebellion to the LORD."
>   And you *forgave* me! All my *guilt is gone*.
>
> (PSALM 32:3–5 NLT, EMPHASIS ADDED)

Please understand, I'm not saying that unconfessed sin is the cause of depression. But we must be honest with God to encounter him, which in turn requires us to deal with contributing factors in our lives, including our sins, in order to overcome depression. God forgave all our sin—past, present, and future—but we still need to walk in a daily relationship with him in which we're completely honest.

When we let go of our past and confess our secrets, we're finally able to face God. As Jacob discovered, no matter how far or fast he ran, all roads led back to God. He tried to make his life work the way he wanted it to work on his own—and failed. But then he realized he could never move forward toward a better future unless he wrestled God. My favorite part of Jacob's story is his fierce determination. He refused to give in until he received God's blessing. It cost him, and his hip injury left him with a limp, but in the process Jacob became Israel—who he was supposed to be.

Some of us spend years and years running from God, resisting his pursuit, and it just won't work. No matter where we go, we sense his presence, receive his generosity and kindness, and hear his gentle voice. We've hardened our hearts and allowed past pains and burdensome secrets to form a barrier. But we will never have rest and peace, we will never get out of our cave, until we let go of our defenses, our anger, and our pride. Like the Israelites, we will never enter our promised land of a more joyful, purposeful future until we repent and turn toward God:

> That is why the Holy Spirit says,
> "Today when you hear his voice,
>> *don't harden your hearts*
> as Israel did when they rebelled,
>> when they tested me in the wilderness.
> There your ancestors tested and tried my patience,
>> even though they saw my miracles for forty years.
> So I was angry with them, and I said,
> 'Their hearts always *turn away from me*.
>> They refuse to do what I tell them.'
> So in my anger I took an oath:
> 'They will *never enter my place of rest*.'"
>> (HEBREWS 3:7–11 NLT, EMPHASIS ADDED)

Sometimes we make connecting with God harder than it needs to be. He asks only that we open our hearts to him. He loves us and knows what we need even better than we know ourselves.

If you're weary of running from your past, of hiding behind a mask to protect your secrets, then it's time to stop pretending. That's what happened to both Jacob and to Elijah.

They had a God encounter that changed everything.

And so can you.

Holy Hide-and-Seek

Once you're done wrestling, it's time to start worshipping.

If you're fighting the good fight and pushing through the darkness, it's not hard to find God. Simply start worshipping and he will find you! God inhabits worship. He's drawn by the openness of our hearts toward him in full, loving surrender. Jesus tells us that "true worshipers will worship the Father in the Spirit and in truth, for they are the kind of worshipers the Father seeks" (John 4:23). This kind of true worship helps us to focus on God and not ourselves, gives him the glory he deserves regardless of how we feel, and helps us to pursue him with our whole heart and soul.

As a grandfather, I recently gained a new perspective on what it means to seek God. There's nothing I enjoy more than playing with my grandkids, and at their young age, they love hide-and-seek. As I learned to choose hiding places that were not right in front of them but not too far away, I wondered if God sometimes does the same thing. I love playing with my grandkids, but I'm not keeping myself from them. I just know how much they enjoy trying to find me!

God never plays games with us, but he likes us to pursue him. If you're having a hard time finding God, just worship him. He is with us and never makes it too hard for us to find him. He's a relational God and loves to be pursued as much as I do when my grandkids spot me behind the couch, squeal with delight, and run into my arms.

They know I am only hiding to be found. God knows we experience a similar special joy when we seek him and discover his presence in our midst.

In story after story in the Bible, we see God reveal his identity when people earnestly looked for him. They would seek him and he would meet them. This is the experience Elijah had when he took the forty-day journey to Mount Horeb. Even though he still retreated to the darkness of the cave, Elijah heard God's voice and stepped forward.

In every situation, when we seek God by worshipping him, we will encounter him. I realize worship may be the last thing we feel like doing when we're battling depression. Which I believe only makes it more special when we wrestle through the resistance and do it anyway. We're fighting to worship, stretching our faith to the breaking point, seeking him despite the darkness of our caves.

Throughout the Bible, we see examples of people struggling but choosing to worship and finding God. No matter what David was experiencing—persecution from King Saul, attacks by lions and bears, guilt from his affair with Bathsheba—he knew that there was always joy to be found in worshipping God. "Be still, and know that I am God' (Psalm 46:10), he wrote, expressing God's invitation to us, because he knew, "In Your presence is fullness of joy" (Psalm 16:11 NKJV).

Worship changes everything.

The prophet Isaiah even described worship as an antidote to depression: "The garment of praise for the spirit of heaviness; that they may be called trees of righteousness, the planting of the LORD, that he may be glorified" (Isaiah 61:3 NKJV). Notice the exchange here, a "spirit of heaviness" is replaced by the "garment of praise" when we worship God.

We live in a time when life feels heavier than ever before. There's a gravity pulling us down. So many demands. Hourly headlines of the latest deaths, crises, protests, crimes, and catastrophes. The constant bombardment takes a toll on our soul.

We must create environments in which we can be close to God. Where we can quiet ourselves and make room for him. Where we can hear the quiet whisper of his Spirit speaking to our hearts. He's right here—closer than we think.

Don't allow your pain and depression to have the last word. They cannot destroy you unless you give up the struggle. Wrestle and worship. Dark moments set up an opportunity for you to step out to the mouth of the cave—and into the light, where you'll not only experience God's loving presence but hear the most important message of your life: "My beloved child, you're only getting started! I've got an assignment for you."

So, as they say on any show you've ever binge-watched:

To be continued!

CHAPTER 12

Stepping into a True Identity

No one can make you feel inferior
without your consent.
—ELEANOR ROOSEVELT

Her memory is sketchy because it happened right before her fifth birthday. But while playing in her backyard near a small mountain village in Colombia, South America, Marina Chapman remembers a sweaty arm grabbing her from behind and placing a hood over her head. She inhaled a strange chemical smell and lost consciousness. She remembers fighting to wake up as she was dragged into the jungle.

As her captor pulled her deeper into the wilderness, branches and thorns scratched her skin. When her abductor finally stopped, he quickly tied her arms. Even as the dark hood stayed on, she felt her clothes being torn off as her assailant did unspeakable things to her little body. Then just as quickly as he had abducted her, he left her there on the ground—arms still tied, hood still on, clothes torn off—to die in the jungle.

Marina couldn't believe she was still alive. After struggling for several hours, she managed to free her hands and remove the hood. With night descending over the dense, tropical foliage, she began to cry, still in shock and terrified by what had happened. The sounds of the jungle grew louder as darkness enveloped her. Marina remained terrified, dozing and shivering throughout the night. Surely someone would rescue her, she thought, as dawn light finally pierced the green canopy overhead.

But no one came. She was so hungry and tired and afraid. Her second night was spent much like the first, trying to remain awake and vigilant amid the cacophony of screeches, hisses, and primal cries. She began to believe she would die there.

The third day something phenomenal happened. A troop of capuchin monkeys saw Marina and, becoming more curious about this new, strange creature, they surrounded her. At first they were hostile, running and charging at her, screaming and hitting her. But after realizing she posed no danger, they settled down. As they casually foraged for food, they wandered away only to return and leave some fruit behind for her to eat.

The next day, they returned. So Marina decided to follow them in hopes of surviving by doing what they did. She began to exist by following a literal "monkey-see, monkey-do" kind of routine. When rain fell, the monkeys caught it in large leaves and drank it, so she did the same. She ate the ripe fruit they discovered, along with certain leaves, seeds, and berries.

Three days turned into a week, a week into a month, and a month turned into years. For more than five years, Marina lived in the jungle with the monkeys. After a while and much practice, Marina could climb up into the canopy of trees with her new family. She didn't speak to another human, had no contact with anyone, and soon her memories of being a little girl faded away. She began to speak the language of the monkeys with grunts, growls, squeaks, and hand motions. She learned to adapt and survived for years by living with the monkeys.

Then one day she noticed something. Scanning the jungle high from her perch on a tree branch, Marina saw light glinting on the ground below. Curious, she raced down to look for the source and discovered something shiny and silvery. She picked it up and tried to bite it, but then turning it over, she looked down and saw a pair of dark eyes looking back at her. Terrified, she threw it down and ran away, assuming it was alive. From a distance, she watched it closely, and when it didn't move, she picked it up again and cautiously looked in the mirror. Her own eyes stared back at her.

For the first time in five years, Marina Chapman saw another human being—*herself*. Even more startling, she realized how different she was from the monkeys or any of the other creatures she had encountered in the jungle. She thought, *I am not a monkey. I am not what they are. I was not made to be what they are. I don't know what I am yet, but I've had a glimpse of who I am now, and I know what I'm not.*

One glimpse of the truth changed the life she had accepted for herself. The mirror revealed who she was supposed to be. The mirror also showed her who she wasn't supposed to be.

Marina went back to the monkeys, but she went back different from before. She returned with an awareness that she was made for more. Never again would she be satisfied living like the monkeys.

Eventually, Marina was found by hunters who took her to the nearest city and traded her to a brothel in return for a parrot. Realizing she was being trained for prostitution, Marina planned her escape and never looked back. Eventually, she wrote a bestselling book, *The Girl with No Name*, describing her life in both the natural and urban jungles of Colombia. Now in her sixties, Marina lives in England where her favorite pastime is, you guessed it, climbing trees—only now with her grandchildren.[1]

Made for More

You and I might not have been raised by monkeys, but we do sometimes lose sight of our true identity in the midst of battling depression. It's only as we get close to God in prayer and look into his Word that we're able to see a true image of God that enables us to view a true image of ourselves—a picture of who God wants us to become.

The apostle Paul beautifully described this dynamic when he wrote, "We all, with unveiled face, beholding as in a mirror the glory of the Lord, are being transformed into the same image from glory to glory, just as by the Spirit of the Lord" (2 Corinthians 3:18 NKJV). In other words, when we remove our veils—whatever prevents us from seeing clearly and being clearly seen—we catch a glimpse of God's glory reflected in who we are. Once we're "unveiled," we have access to God. And as we get closer to him, we are changed into his image—the essence of who we were created to be in the first place.

But here's the problem: we're all living in a jungle. And the jungle wants to tell us who we are, what we look like, and what to do. It rewards us when we follow the monkey-see, monkey-do conformity of those around us. We're encouraged to live a life of self-indulgence, self-exaltation, self-gratification, or any number of other self-defeating behaviors simply because everybody else does.

But then we catch a glimpse of ourselves in a new mirror. We come to church or talk to someone who's not playing the monkey game, or read a book like this one, and we see clearly who we are supposed to be. Like Marina Chapman, we realize we were made to be so much more. When we catch a divine glimpse of who we really are, we realize, "I was made for more than hanging out in the jungle like everyone else. I was made for more than depression. I was made for *immortality*."

Too many of us have settled for a jungle life. We let our friends tell us who we are, we let Hollywood tell us what beauty is, we let pop music stars tell us what love is. We let social media dictate the clothes we wear and the products we buy. We let the jungle define our values and morals and choices. We do all this to become who we think we want to be. Chasing after a monkey's life of fleeting happiness and momentary pleasure.

In one of her many interviews, Marina Chapman told a columnist, "One day, you just accept the world . . . and you just carry on without thinking about your future."[2] We often accept our world the same way and resign ourselves to an endless chase in the jungle. But it doesn't have to be this way.

One of the keys to getting out of depression is knowing who you are. Specifically, your purpose and assignment in life. This is your reason for living. When you're in the grip of depression, your focus is naturally on stopping the depression. But what if the cure you need isn't about *stopping* something but about *starting* something?

Instead of focusing on what's happened to you and who you've become and how you feel, what if you focused instead on who you are—who you *really* are? Who the God of the universe created you to be?

Again, it's important to acknowledge that some of us struggle with depression because of genetics, biology, and other issues that have nothing to do with lifestyle patterns, traumatic events, or substance abuse. And in those cases, depression needs to be treated in the same way we would treat any other sickness. However, studies also reveal that depression and anxiety emerge from the things that have happened to us or things we've allowed in our lives. Again, this is actually good news because it means we have some measure of control over our response—we have the ability to change.

With God's help, we can discover new ways to see what happened to us in the past and trust that God can somehow redeem even the most painful losses. With his Spirit guiding and directing us, we can find the power to change habits and get out of the jungle ruts in which we've been living.

First, though, we have to reconsider how we see ourselves.

The Stories We Tell

One thing I've learned after pastoring people for almost forty years is this: People will *feel* based on the narrative they *believe* about themselves. Their emotions follow the story they tell themselves, and they make choices and develop default behavior patterns that fit their narratives. If they have connected the dots of their life's events, especially in childhood, to create a story that's not true, then they get stuck. And sooner or later, they get depressed.

For example, if a child received hugs from her dad and praise from her mom only when she made good grades or excelled in sports, she logically concludes that she has to win and achieve in order to be loved. Without the maturity and neurological development to know otherwise, she develops a narrative that she is unworthy of love unless she earns it. She carries this false belief into adulthood but becomes depressed when she exhausts herself—at home, at work, at church—and still doesn't feel appreciated, seen, or loved for who she is rather than what she does.

Or maybe another child suffered the loss of a father to illness, divorce, or abandonment at an early age. He's raised by a mom who is overwhelmed by going back to work, paying bills, and parenting in the midst of her own devastating grief. So this little boy begins to feel inferior. He wonders how he will ever learn to be a man without a father or strong male role model. He assumes that something must be wrong with him because his father isn't there for him. He goes on to college, gets a great job, and marries a woman who loves him, but doesn't feel comfortable in his own skin or confident as a man because he secretly believes he doesn't have what it takes to be a husband, father, and leader.

Depending on the events in our lives, the stories we tell ourselves can have an impact that's more than emotional or psychological. In his bestselling book *The Body Keeps the Score*, Dr. Bessel van der Kolk shares his findings after more than thirty years of treating combat veterans, abuse survivors, and lifelong addicts. As the title of his book suggests, his study reveals how trauma of any kind changes our bodies and our brains. Our minds and bodies are so connected that our body keeps a physiological record of reactions to traumatic moments, almost as an imprint. For example, a child placed in foster care might assimilate well with his new family for many months but then start to act out as the anniversary of a major trauma, such as being taken from an abusive situation and placed into care, rolls around. While his mind forgot the date and timeline of previous pain, his body kept the score of his traumatic past.

We may have forgotten details or fail to consciously recognize the trauma we've suffered, but our bodies remember. And yet, we may not receive or recognize the message our bodies send us. There's a kind of logic in seeing how our stories started and where we are in them now.

To alleviate or eliminate the internal impact of external trauma and the stories we tell ourselves about it, we must look in the right mirror. And the right mirror is what God says about us. He created us, so he should know. Otherwise, we will continue to cling to false beliefs instead of focusing on who we really are. Our bodies hold on to elements of the past until our spirits make a course correction.

If you've been looking in the wrong mirrors, you're going to see distorted reflections of who you are. You'll see images that have been defined by your environment or culture or family or words other people have said about you. These images will be based on data that seems to make sense to you even though it is incredibly flawed, subjective, and inaccurate. Simply put, none of those images can ever give you an accurate picture of who you really are.

Why?

Because the only One qualified to *define* you is the One who *created* you.

What you believe about yourself is foundational, and the real you can only be found in connecting with the One who made you. When you know who you are, your feelings may sometimes lag behind but, ultimately, they will line up with the holy truth about who you really are.

If you want to stop depression, start using a new mirror.

Message in the Mirror

In the Disney classic *Snow White*, the Evil Queen relied on her magic mirror to tell her what she wanted to hear. In her insecurity, she daily asked, "Mirror, mirror, on the wall, who is the fairest of them all?" She was looking for validation, which we all need and want, but looking for it in the wrong place. Which explains her vendetta against Snow White, whose beauty so easily outshined her own.

While most of us grew up identifying with Snow White or Prince Charming, the truth is that we're all much more like Her Misguided Majesty. We're all looking for validation somewhere, but most of us are asking the wrong mirror to give us what we want. So, like the Evil Queen, we begin hunting down our own personal Snow White, whoever or whatever threatens the source of our validation. We may not poison apples, but we often do whatever it takes to secure our identity.

The truth is, most of us feel insecure sometimes, but some of us feel insecure most of the time. It often goes back to the kind of childhood we had. Past traumas as well as recent experiences of failure or rejection influence how secure we feel. Loneliness, social anxiety, perfectionism, destructive criticism—these can all evolve into negative beliefs about ourselves and contribute to massive insecurity.

If you want to see clearly who God intended you to be, you first have to step away from the false mirrors you've been relying on for affirmation. Where do you look for your validation each day? What and who defines your identity and how you think about yourself?

Before you answer, let's look at three mirrors that reflect messages back to us and commonly lead to depression. Those mirrors are mistakes and wrong choices, social pressure, and inferiority.

1. Mistakes and Wrong Choices

When you look in the mirror of mistakes or bad decisions, you believe, "I am what I did." You're basing your identity on your actions.

As the father of five kids, I recall plenty of times when they did things they were not supposed to do. After discovery, there was the dreaded confrontation followed by the requisite discipline. Most of the time, the kids would feel upset, ashamed, disappointed in themselves, and afraid they had become what they had done. In fact, several years ago when one of my sons was arrested for underage drinking and I told him we needed to talk, he clearly expected the worst. However, instead of giving him an angry lecture, I reminded him of the truth of his identity.

"That's what you did," I told him, "but that's not who you are."

And I'm telling you the same truth today: *You are not what you did.*

Your decisions reflect what you did, but they are not who you are. They can become who you are, though, if you don't change them.

2. Social Pressure

The mirror of social pressure says, "I am who they say I am." This happens when we let other people define us and put labels on us. The loser. The addict. The achiever. The trendsetter. The loner. The pretty one. The joker. Peer pressure then guides our steps, and we idolize social standards for a sense of identity. We take comfort when we conform and fit in, and panic when others reject, abandon, or exclude us.

This mirror provides the worst, most inaccurate reflection of who you really are. Why? Because most people will put you down simply to elevate themselves! Which means your sense of self goes up and down on a daily basis, leaving you even more frustrated, confused, and insecure. It's like being a kid in school all over again, riding the waves of who's in and who's out among the various cliques.

3. INFERIORITY

The looking glass of inferiority says, "I am not enough." So many of us have completely unrealistic expectations for ourselves and for how life should be. And when the disappointments from these two sets of expectations collide, we assume it's because we're somehow inadequate and therefore to blame.

This was my mirror growing up. In middle school (or junior high school, as we called it then), I was often bullied by my peers. I wasn't athletic or popular, and I felt like I could never live up to the social norms and expectations required to be accepted by my classmates.

My sense of inferiority followed me into adulthood. Even after I became a Christian and pursued pastoral ministry, I never felt like I was enough. Looking around at other pastors and leaders, I always saw how they were so much better than I was. They were more talented, smarter, more committed, more passionate about their faith, had more experience or a better education.

I still struggle with insecurity. From time to time, I feel like I cannot live up to everyone's expectations. Even today as I go out on stage to preach, a little voice pipes up in my mind and says, *There are so many people who are smarter than you watching and listening—what do you possibly have to offer them?*

But what I've realized is that no one else has these expectations of me. The expectations that torment me are the ones I've created in my own mind. I'm the one setting impossibly high expectations day after day. I'm the one setting myself up to fail.

I'm the one relying on a distorted reflection.

All three of these mirrors—mistakes / wrong choices, social pressure, inferiority—have major flaws in the reflections they cast back at us. Like those crazy funhouse mirrors at carnivals and theme parks, they distort who we really are. If we continue relying on our failures, our peers, or our insecurities to define us, we will likely end up in a spiral of depression.

A New Mirror

To see ourselves accurately, we must look to a new mirror. And to find out who we are supposed to be, we must ask the One who made us. God created us, and he's the only One who knows who we are. So we must look to him to catch a glimpse of our true identity. We must rely on his truth, his Word, and his Spirit to reveal who we really are.

My hope for you is that you would catch a glimpse of how God sees you. Because if you look into the mirror God has for you, nothing will ever look the same again. You will realize that you've been living your life without seeing the truth about who you are, who God is, and what your life is all about. When you look into God's loving mirror of truth, what you will see is that you are forgiven, you are healed, and you are called.

1. You Are Forgiven

Accepting God's amazing grace shatters the false messages of distorted mirrors and allows the reality of God's love and mercy to open your eyes. Then you realize that God isn't mad at you or breathing down your neck to punish you for your mistakes. He loves you more than you can fathom.

When I was growing up, I formed an image of God that bears a striking resemblance to the Wizard of Oz—a grumpy, fear-inducing old tyrant who demanded my obedience. I believed he would forgive me and grant me what I needed and wanted as long as I toed the line and performed for him. But I could never do enough and get it right—trying to please the Wizard only left me frustrated.

Then one of the greatest revelations of my life changed everything. I realized God—the living and holy Creator, not a creation of my skewed imagination—loved me no matter what I did or didn't do. He loved me so much, in fact, that he forgave all my sins. He loved me so much that he gave up his most precious Son to live and die as a man on this earth so that the penalty for my sins could be paid once and for all.

The promise of John 3:16 broke the false mirror of my inferiority once and for all: "For God so loved the world that he gave his one and only Son, that whoever believes in him shall not perish but have eternal life." My understanding of God changed as I shifted from performing religion for God to living in an intimate relationship with God. Living the Christian faith went from something I had to do, to someone I desired more than anything else. No longer motivated by escaping hell, I longed to know God and to be known by him.

God loves me, gave his Son for me, and placed me in his family as his beloved child. This truth defines me. I was no longer a monkey in the jungle, but a person created in God's image. I had glimpsed who I really am and it changed the way I saw everything—including myself.

Marina Chapman revealed that once she glimpsed her own face in that mirror, she was ruined for monkey life. She wasn't who she thought she was. Although she climbed back to the top of the trees, she realized, "I don't belong here."

When we catch a glimpse of who we really are, it shatters old, distorted images.

When I got saved, the first thing I did was break up with my girlfriend, Darla. I already knew she and I were looking in different mirrors, but suddenly, I viewed our relationship differently. I also told all my closest friends that I was following Jesus and would no longer be living by the rules of the jungle. I tried to reach them so they could join me in realizing who God had made them to be, but they mostly weren't interested. Many of them were surprised when I actually did what I said and got out of the jungle.

You need to make a similar break with whatever jungle you might be living in. You no longer belong in the jungle, living by its rules and norms. God calls us to influence our environment but not to allow it to influence us. We are to be salt and light, not monkeys in the darkness. We're told, "Therefore, if anyone is in Christ, he is a new creation; old things have passed away; behold, all things have become new" (2 Corinthians 5:17 NKJV).

2. YOU ARE HEALED

When you glimpse the truth, here's the second message you'll see reflected: *you are healed*. It's a phrase that usually makes us think of sickness, but healing is not just about physical wellness. A disease is any place where you are "dis-eased"—unsettled, anxious, afraid. When you've been living in the jungle, your emotions, your choices, and your self-image all become tainted by disease.

Even when we've left the jungle behind, a little of it can still linger within us. We struggle to see ourselves the way God sees us. Others' lies still echo in our minds. We're tempted to run back to old familiar habits even when we know they're harmful.

Living in your true, God-given identity often requires healing your soul. You invite God to make every part of your life his, restoring what's been broken, healing what still hurts. This is what righteousness means. It doesn't mean some kind of holy perfection—it means righting the wrongs. God wants to make things right in you: "God made him who had no sin to be sin for us, so that in him we might become the righteousness of God" (2 Corinthians 5:21).

It often takes time and patience, but you might be surprised how God will right these wrongs. As I shared, I've struggled with insecurity much of my life, so the prospect of being in front of other people and preaching did not come naturally. When I failed my speech class in college, it only confirmed my insecurity. But I kept trusting God, looking in his mirror rather than my own, studying his Word, and delivering the messages he gave me to share from the pulpit. It was uncomfortable and scary at first, and often it still is, but I've kept going because I look in his mirror and try to glimpse what he sees. It's the only reason I can speak in front of thousands of people today.

It's important to remember that healing rarely happens in an instant. Instead, it happens as a process that takes place over time and may best be completed under the care of a mental health professional. Some of us feel shame when we have repeatedly and wholeheartedly asked the Lord to rid us of our depression and it hasn't happened. Just because God hasn't removed it from our lives doesn't mean he's not in the midst of it with us. Sometimes we need ongoing help reframing how we see God and understanding how he sees us in order to break through symptoms of our depression and anxiety.

We are changed little by little, from glory to glory, step by step. So we keep praying, reading the Bible, going to church and participating, and we begin seeing ourselves differently. We change as we see a different vision. Sometimes we may notice a shift and realize God is calling us to something new. This is good! He helps us work on one area and then reveals another. It takes time.

You don't have to do anything except take a look at the truth.

Then take the next step God reveals to you, whatever it may be. You don't have to remain bound to old habits or enslaved by depression. *You are healed in Jesus' name!*

3. YOU ARE CALLED

The third truth you will glimpse in God's mirror is this: *you are called.*

God created you on purpose for a purpose. He calls you to use your unique gifts in ways no one else can serve. You are his handiwork, a one-of-a-kind living, breathing, functional work of art. This isn't merely my poetic opinion, it's God Word: "For we are God's masterpiece. He has created us anew in Christ Jesus, so we can do the good things he planned for us long ago" (Ephesians 2:10 NLT).

When I was nineteen, I went to a church camp at Paul B. Johnson State Park about ten miles south of Hattiesburg, Mississippi. In one of our assemblies, the speaker prayed over me and spoke into my future. It felt prophetic, especially as I look back on it now. How else could he know, right? He gave me a glimpse of my future that was both encouraging and a little overwhelming: "One day you will reach so many people, like the stars in the sky." That day, in that moment, I felt the presence of God. I saw myself leading people into worship. I got a glimpse of who I could be.

I remembered that moment some years later when I caught another glimpse of my calling while standing at the top of a hill in Birmingham, Alabama. I was there to watch an LSU baseball game and had stopped at a coffee shop because I arrived earlier than expected and had some time to kill. As I stood there sipping my latte and staring out over six lanes of cars all bumper to bumper on Highway 280, I sensed God saying, "One day you will pastor the people sitting there in that traffic jam." His voice scared me because it seemed loud and almost audible. *Where did that come from?* Had to be God!

That afternoon, I caught a glimpse of ministry in Alabama, enough of one that I moved there from Louisiana. I didn't know how to plant a church, how to lead one, let alone how to serve in the ways I'm now so blessed to serve. I kept answering God's call, though, and following those glimpses, which were holy breadcrumbs leading me where God wanted me next.

God wants to give you a glimpse of who you really are and what you're uniquely designed to do. If you don't believe me, then I dare you to believe him: "'I know the plans I have for you,' declares the LORD, 'plans to prosper you and not to harm you, plans to give you hope and a future'" (Jeremiah 29:11).

You might have a sense of the call God is placing on your life right now. Maybe you hear the whisper of his Spirit revealing your next step. Can you glimpse what he has for you? Do you realize that's who you really are?

You are forgiven.

You are healed.

You are called.

And you are also *blessed*. The word *blessing* carries with it a sense of prosperity, although that word has become tarnished. Blessing isn't money and financial abundance but simply a sense of divine momentum, a push forward. Blessing means God is on your side so you can make a difference in the world.

God wants to help you make a difference. That's what he made you to do. And you don't have to do it on your own. He's with you every step of the way. As he leads you, you have nothing to fear.

Glimpsing his truth, you can change the world.

CHAPTER 13

Stepping into a New Assignment

> People have enough to live by but nothing to
> live for; they have the means but no meaning.
> —Viktor Frankl

When you face the worst in life, how do you keep going?
Why do you keep going?

Imagine watching your loved ones, friends, and neighbors being herded like cattle onto trains that will take them to their final destinations, where they will suffer torturous deaths.

Imagine being separated from your spouse, from your children, from your aging parents and not knowing if you will ever see them alive again.

Imagine feeling the kicks and shoves of sneering guards as you're crammed into boxcars and holding cells, shoulder to shoulder with countless others.

Imagine hearing the screams, the sobs, the pleading voices and desperate shrieks of children, fathers and mothers, brothers and sisters, husbands and wives torn apart from one another.

Imagine smelling the scent of sweat and blood, urine and feces, the acrid smoke of seared flesh, the fetid stench of decay.

Imagine being stripped of your identity, losing everything you've worked so hard to attain, tortured until you no longer feel the pain, and starved until you're too weak to stand.

Could you survive such unimaginable suffering? Could you endure the injustice of knowing your anguish results only from your captors' passionate hatred of your race?

No matter how hard we try, we simply cannot fathom the horrors of the Holocaust. But Holocaust survivor, psychiatrist, and humanitarian Viktor Frankl experienced them firsthand. He endured conditions that defy comprehension. But then he later drew on those same traumatic experiences to find meaning and hope, and to help millions of others do the same. His story has always fascinated me, and his theory of logotherapy provides significant insights to help us win the battle over depression.

Significance in Suffering

The people who inspire us most are often those who have suffered most. Viktor Frankl's life certainly embodies this truth.[1] Prior to World War II, he had spent his life studying psychology, philosophy, neurology, and psychiatry. He corresponded with Sigmund Freud and apprenticed with Alfred Adler, focusing on the fundamental meaning of life, both individually and socially.

By the time he was a twenty-one-year-old graduate student, Frankl began writing and lecturing about how values and meaning in life relate to mental health. One translation of the Greek word *logos* is "meaning," and so he coined the term *logotherapy* to describe his study of human motivation and how the presence or absence of meaning affects our responses to suffering.

Frankl was in his midthirties and practicing at a clinic for Jewish patients in Vienna when war broke out and Adolf Hitler's Nazi government annexed Austria. As German forces took control, Frankl risked his own life to prevent mentally ill patients from being euthanized. In 1941, while still in Vienna, he met and married his first wife, Tilly Grosser, just as the Nazis began imprisoning Jewish citizens at various concentration camps. Shortly after their marriage, Mrs. Frankl became pregnant but was forced by German doctors to abort the baby.

In 1942, Viktor and Tilly were arrested and deported, along with Viktor's parents, to a processing center near Prague. His sister, Stella, managed to escape to Australia while his brother, Walter, and his sister-in-law traveled to Italy in hopes of fleeing Europe as well. Frankl's unpublished manuscript for a seminal book on logotherapy, *The Doctor and the Soul*, was destroyed at the deportation center. A few months later, his father died from exhaustion.

After nearly two years, Viktor, his wife, and his mother were sent to the infamous Auschwitz-Birkenau concentration camp in German-occupied Poland. There, unknown to him at the time, his sixty-five-year-old mother was killed in the gas chamber. Viktor was then transferred to a labor camp, where he contracted typhoid fever, and Tilly was transferred to the Bergen-Belsen camp in northern Germany.

US troops finally liberated prisoners, including Viktor, in April 1945 as the Allied Forces ended the war. Desperate to find Tilly, Frankl traveled the dangerous journey to Vienna only to receive horrible news—his wife, his mother, his brother, and his brother's wife had all been murdered. Despite such devastating losses, Frankl vowed to persevere.

In 1946, he became director of the Vienna Neurological Polyclinic, a position he held for twenty-five years, and immediately rewrote the manuscript for his lost book, adding a chapter on the psychology of prisoners in concentration campus. As one of the first books published in postwar Europe, the first edition sold out in a matter of days. Encouraged by its reception, Frankl wrote his next book right away—in only nine days—a psychological and philosophical treatise on human suffering later published in English as *Man's Search for Meaning*.

In 1948, Frankl finished his PhD in philosophy and went on to serve as a full professor at the University of Vienna. He married again, and he and his wife, Eleonore Schwindt, had a daughter, Gabriele. Frankl traveled the world, teaching, lecturing, and writing on the theme of finding hope and significance in the midst of life's most unimaginable suffering. He died in 1997 at the age of ninety-two from heart failure, but the heart of his work and his mission lives on.

Viktor Frankl's suffering became the catalyst for actualizing his significance.

Liberty and Responsibility

During a stint as guest professor at Harvard University in 1961, Frankl commented on the emphasis American culture placed on personal freedom by remarking, "The Statue of Liberty on the East Coast should be supplemented by a Statue of Responsibility on the West Coast."[2] His observation still resonates today, not just for Americans but for all of us trying to overcome depression in our current age of anxiety.

The freedoms we enjoy also come with responsibilities. We are entrusted by God with free will, and so we have the privilege of choosing how we live and what we're living for. Free will also comes with responsibility, which means we always have choices even when we don't like them. Frankl wrote, "When we are no longer able to change a situation, we are challenged to change ourselves."[3]

Frankl believed that Freud's theory about what motivates human beings—various kinds of gratifications—was misguided. In a German concentration camp, deprived of virtually all freedom and pleasures, Frankl became convinced that the secret to life was in finding meaning. And when human beings lack meaning in life, they dull the pain of meaninglessness by pursuing pleasure.

With this premise in mind, Frankl treated patients suffering from depression and suicidal tendencies based on three logotherapeutic tenets:

- Everyone needs to do some type of meaningful work, to do something with their life that matters.
- Everyone needs a community of friends who love them unconditionally. A person cannot be healthy alone.
- Everyone needs to take whatever suffering they experience and find something positive about it.

Not a single patient under Frankl's care committed suicide.

After World War II, many of those he treated were concentration camp survivors like himself. They struggled with the crushing grief of unbearable loss and guilt for surviving when their loved ones, along with millions of others, did not. They wrestled with rage at the arbitrary nature of such heinous injustice and callous brutality. They grappled with how to move forward in any positive direction after being forever changed by the horrors they had experienced.

Frankl's message, supported by the credibility of his own suffering and the authority of his personal and professional training, sparked hope. He asserted that he would use his life to make a difference and try to help alleviate others' suffering—and that each one of us, no matter what we have been through, faces the same existential choice. Because if he allowed himself to hibernate in a cave of despair, then his survival would be in vain. Frankl refused to allow the evil that destroyed his family and caused his suffering to silence him.

When we battle depression, we face the same choice.

Will we allow our pain to consume us? Or will we live for something bigger, something meaningful that sustains us even in our grief, depression, and anxiety?

Viktor Frankl knew that the opposite of depression isn't happiness—it's meaning and purpose. So many of us have what Frankl termed a "narrative void," a life without meaning. We can't make sense of why some events happen and others don't. We contemplate our existence and return again and again to the raw and nagging question, "Why?"

But such ruminations often lead back to depression. In the face of the inexplicable, there are no answers. When life doesn't turn out the way we want, we often play the victim card by assigning blame to others—parents, a spouse, those who hurt us. Doing so may provide temporary emotional relief, but it won't sustain us and help us find our God-given purpose.

If you don't believe me, just ask Elijah.

Back to Beersheba

You'll recall we left Elijah at the mouth of his cave on Mount Horeb. God had led him there after restoring him with rest and nourishment. And after demonstrating his power and might, the Lord whispered to Elijah, who responded by covering his face and stepping forward. He then had a conversation with God that began with his response to God's question, "What are you doing here, Elijah?"

He replied, "I have been very zealous for the LORD God Almighty. The Israelites have rejected your covenant, torn down your altars, and put your prophets to death with the sword. I am the only one left, and now they are trying to kill me too." (1 Kings 19:14)

The first thing I notice here is the way Elijah perceived his predicament. "I have been very zealous for the LORD," he said before listing all that's gone wrong and contributed to his depression. There's an implicit logic here: Elijah thought he had served God effectively, and therefore he felt like God owed him something. I've felt that way. I serve and minister and worship and obey and do everything in my power to strengthen my faith and deepen my love of God. Wouldn't it be great then if God rewarded me for trying to do my part?

Elijah listed his grievances once again. He was discouraged because it felt like his efforts were in vain—the Israelites did not repent and continued to reject God's covenant. From there, Elijah slid into a pity party, "I'm the only one left!"

Then it was the Lord's turn to speak, and here is the first thing he said: "Go back the way you came, and go to the Desert of Damascus" (1 Kings 19:15). The Lord then went on to give Elijah detailed instructions about what he was to do next, which Elijah followed (vv. 15–19).

Did you notice that God did not comment on the issues Elijah complained about? Fascinating! Instead, God reminded Elijah of his calling by giving him a new assignment and telling him, "Go back the way you came." I suspect Elijah may not have wanted to hear this. After running away, he blamed circumstances and others for his condition, even to the point of wanting to end his life. And yet, God sent him right back the way he came. This required returning to Beersheba, which literally means "the well of the oath," a fitting spot for Elijah to renew his commitment to serve God.

This directive to go back the way we came—to return to the places we have avoided or written off as terminal failures—applies as much to us today as it did to Elijah thousands of years ago. God's desire for you—and for every discouraged and depressed person—is to get us back into a life of influence and meaning. "But I've failed," you might say. "I tried to do what I thought God wanted and nothing has changed."

So what? Remember, it's a process, a journey, one that often feels like a wrestling match.

Everyone fails. Everyone becomes discouraged and depressed at some point. We all lose our momentum and feel like we can't keep going. We tend to look at our failure and think, *I've blown it. I give up. I obviously can't do this, so why try again?* We think we're disqualified from ever influencing others when the fact is that we are the only one believing that lie.

Because terminal failure and disqualification is not how God works.

When discouragement and depression happen, what is God's desire for you and me? He wants us to heal and restore us so we can get back in the game. After God connected with Elijah and restored their relationship, he told Elijah to go back the way he came because he still had a purpose for Elijah's life. In fact, there is never a time you and I are without a God-given purpose.

We can always continue to serve God in whatever way he asks.

We're not finished until he says so.

The Power of Purpose

Without a dream, revelation, or purpose, we perish.

Perhaps not physically—at least not right away—but emotionally.

And when we've lost our reason to live, we think it doesn't matter how we live.

We've considered this truth before, but allow me to jog your memory. The Bible says, "Where there is no vision, the people perish" (Proverbs 29:18 kjv). The niv translation renders it this way: "Where there is no revelation, people cast off restraint."

Simply put, without a sense of meaningful purpose, why bother?

Perhaps one of the most vivid illustrations of this truth comes from the life of King David. David fell into sin when he wasn't pursuing his purpose. While other leaders were off to war, fighting to preserve and protect what they believed in, David was wandering aimlessly around his palace. He ended up on the rooftop in the cool of the evening where he spotted a bathing beauty named Bathsheba.

Basically, David was at home doing nothing when he should have been fighting a battle that mattered. He wouldn't have committed adultery had he been where his purpose demanded he be, leading on the front lines of a battle. He certainly wouldn't have had the opportunity to spot Bathsheba bathing.

When we lose sight of our purpose—when we lack a clear vision of who we are and what we are called to do—we make bad choices.

That's certainly been my experience. With the luxury of hindsight, I can trace back at least five significant bouts of depression when I struggled with my direction and lacked vision for my life. My choices during those times weren't necessarily sinful, but without a clear sense of purpose, I focused on the wrong things and felt stuck in place. On the other hand, when I caught the wind in my sails, I experienced a renewed sense of purpose and a restored clarity.

In the Old Testament, the Hebrew word used for "dream" is closely connected to the word that means to be "healthy" or "restored." We're told, "When the Lord restored the fortunes of Zion, we were like those who dreamed. Our mouths were filled with laughter, our tongues with songs of joy" (Psalm 126:1–2). Restoration includes new dreams, a renewed sense of purposeful living.

Every time I begin having dreams for the future again, I always feel healthier. My prayer life is better, I feel more content, and I'm aware of enjoying the journey each day. When I'm distracted and derailed by circumstances, overwhelming emotions, and false assumptions, I sink into the pain of regret. I start blaming and shaming.

In the last few years, I've faced several situations, some of which I've shared with you, that caused my spirit to sink. In each case, I've been able to rise up and step forward again because God gave me a new assignment, just as he did with Elijah. One example is the assignment to launch Highlands College, our endeavor to provide teaching and ministry training programs to young adults who are called into vocational ministry. I love learning and being able to share what I've learned with others. My soul does cartwheels when I'm able to teach a class or share what God has placed on my heart at chapel.

The apostle Paul experienced something similar when he had all kinds of reasons to be depressed and discouraged about his life and his ministry—persecution, assaults, arrest, jail time, shipwrecks, snake bites, you name it. But Paul's purpose in life gave him the strength to suffer, to endure, and to persevere. He explained how we can experience the same peace and perspective even when life seems upside down:

> Therefore we do not lose heart. Though outwardly we are wasting away, yet inwardly we are being renewed day by day. For our light and momentary troubles are achieving for us an eternal glory that far outweighs them all. So we fix our eyes not on what is seen, but on what is unseen, since what is seen is temporary, but what is unseen is eternal. (2 Corinthians 4:16–18)

Paul knew that it matters where our eyes are fixed. If we focus on ourselves, we're in trouble. We only compound the intensity of our depression. But if we focus on our God-given purpose, we discover the strength and energy we need to step forward. I'm convinced that the quickest way to defeat depression is by redirecting our attention from ourselves to the needs of other people. When we give ourselves in ministry to others, God gives us his power to live out our purpose.

Purpose in Your Pain

So how do we get past the crippling emotions of depression and step into our God-given assignments? Especially when we don't feel like moving a muscle in the midst of overwhelming emotions and out-of-control circumstances? We can start by using two strategies.

First, we accept the fact that life is not fair—at least, not from an earthly, human perspective. Anytime you think you should have been treated differently and more fairly, you're only setting yourself up for more disappointment. The Bible is clear about this: "[God] causes his sun to rise on the evil and the good, and sends rain on the righteous and the unrighteous" (Matthew 5:45). And yet, even in our most painful situations, life can always have meaning.

This brings us to the second strategy, which echoes Viktor Frankl's logotherapy: we find purpose—not logical explanations, clearer analysis, or deeper regret—in our pain. If you're going through something hard, try to find your purpose in the midst of it. For example, if a family member is going through medical treatments for a disease, your purpose in that season might be to devote yourself to supporting that person. Even when you're worried, afraid of what might happen, and feel guilty for the disruptions in your normal routines, show up for them anyway. Focus on what it must be like for them to go through this scary experience and how disruptive this disease has been in every area of their lives. Think about what you can do to offer comfort, love, hope, peace, and support. Think of their pain as greater than your own.

The apostle Paul had suffered incredible hardship, and yet he knew that he could use what he learned from God during those times to make a difference in the lives of others. "God is our merciful Father and the source of all comfort," he wrote, "He comforts us in all our troubles so that we can comfort others. When they are troubled, we will be able to give them the same comfort God has given us" (2 Corinthians 1:3–4 NLT).

When you are struggling, God makes a difference in you.

Then he uses you to make a difference in the lives of others.

When you are struggling in your marriage, who would you rather spend time with—someone who has been through a divorce and is willing to share what God has taught them through it, or someone who has never been married? More often than not, your ministry comes from your pain. God wants to use what you've been through to help someone else find their way.

Ultimately, your pain is either a jail that imprisons you or a school that empowers you.

Remember, you have been given freedom to find meaning. No matter what happens, no one can ever take away your freedom to choose your response. Remember what Viktor Frankl said: "Between the stimulus and the response there is a space, and in that space is your power and your freedom." You have a choice. When you embrace the choice you have to transform your suffering into significance, you can create something beautiful from the burden you bear.

Late in life, Viktor Frankl finally acted on a dream he had his entire life—to pilot a plane. In his midsixties, he took flying lessons and earned his solo flight certificate.

Frankl knew it was never too late to dream.

Dreams pull you out of the black-and-white shadows of the cave by adding color, light, and texture to your life's purpose.

Holy Cow

In the book *Lost Connections*, which I've cited previously, journalist Johann Hari interviewed a South African psychiatrist named Dr. Derek Summerfield.[4] In the course of their conversation, Summerfield mentioned that he happened to be in Cambodia in 2001 as part of a medical team who had traveled there to train doctors on how to use antidepressants for patients suffering from depression. At the time, most Cambodian doctors, especially in smaller villages, had not heard of these drugs, Summerfield explained, and so they asked a lot of questions about how such meds worked.

Summerfield recalled one situation in which he explained antidepressants only to be told by some Cambodian doctors, "We don't need these because we already have our own antidepressants."

"Really? What do you mean? What are you using?" Summerfield asked. He assumed the Cambodian doctors were referring to herbal remedies or meditative practices, so Summerfield was quite surprised when they told him a story instead.

As it happened, a farmer in their community was working his rice fields one day when an undetected land mine went off. The farmer lost his leg in the blast but soon recovered and was given a prosthetic leg. When he returned to his rice fields, however, he found it awkward and painful to slog through the wet paddies, especially where the mine had exploded only weeks prior.

After a few attempts, the man refused to go back to working his fields and became so despondent that he cried all day. When the farmer got to the point that he would no longer get out of bed in the morning, one of his loved ones called for help. So the Cambodian doctors visited the man, asked him questions, and then listened as he shared his depression and grief. They realized that the farmer's response made total sense in light of the trauma he had experienced and the collateral losses he suffered along with losing his leg.

"Then we gave him an antidepressant," one of the Cambodian doctors explained.

"What did you prescribe?" asked Summerfield, intrigued.

"We thought about the farmer's situation and bought him a cow. Because with a cow, he could be a dairy farmer and wouldn't have to work in the rice fields. He could sit fairly comfortably to milk the cow and take his time feeding and caring for it. And it worked! After a couple of weeks, the man stopped crying and no longer felt depressed. So you see, we already know about this thing called an antidepressant!"

Much to Dr. Summerfield's delight, his Cambodian colleagues instinctively knew how to be present with the injured farmer in his depression and how to find a way to restore his purpose. They knew that when people have a purpose that enables them to make a contribution to their community, they feel significant.

What they did for this rice farmer is the same thing God did for Elijah—both the farmer and Elijah got new assignments, which gave them renewed purpose.

The key to getting out of our caves of depression is to connect with something more compelling than what we're going through. We all need meaning and a sense of making a difference in our world.

Are you listening for God's voice so you can hear his next assignment for you?

Take a step forward. He's got a new mission waiting that only you can accomplish.

An assignment that will not only change *you* but change the *world*!

CHAPTER 14

Stepping into Relational Strength

*Look carefully at the closest associations in your
life, for that is the direction you are headed.*
—KEVIN EIKENBERRY

Hey, I'm just checking on you. How are you? No, how are you *really?*"

I can't tell you how many times I've gotten calls that begin just like this. Incredible friends, mentors, spiritual fathers, and family members touch base to see how I'm doing, either because they know what I'm going through or feel led by the Holy Spirit to call and check on me. Knowing how much such connections mean, I try to do the same for my family, my staff, pastors whom I pastor, and friends who mean so much to me. Even when I don't feel like talking or have to muster the energy to take or make a call, I know how vitally important it is to do so.

Because relationships provide the best insurance against cave-ins.

When others prevent me from going dark and shutting them out, they keep me involved and aware of more than just myself. They remind me of what's true—about myself, about others, about my purpose, about God. Consequently, I'm convinced God builds his kingdom relationally. His design for our health and protection is centered on family and close friends who love us unconditionally and point us toward his truth.

Which explains why the enemy attacks our relationships so relentlessly. If he can destroy our connections with others, he cuts a crucial lifeline God designed to keep us healthy, whole, and out of the cave of depression. When others disappoint, hurt, exclude, or betray us, we naturally pull away. But isolating ourselves and stewing in our pain never help us heal or move forward. Only forgiveness, grace, and love can sustain us in our relationships.

Otherwise, we let our anger and bitterness fester and poison us. We want to give up on others or hurt them the way they have hurt us. Our depression then causes us to feel isolated and lonely—and when we feel this way, we usually withdraw even more, going deeper into our caves because we believe the enemy's lies that no one cares, no one understands, and no one can help us. But no matter how intense those feelings may be or how much evidence our mind supplies to support our belief, it's still not true.

Others do care about us.

There are people who understand what we're experiencing.

And they can help us—if we let them.

The Company You Keep

I'm very aware of how fortunate I am to have such life-giving relationships. It sounds too good to be true, but I'm astonished by the privilege I've enjoyed most of my life to know some of the absolute best people ever. Now, don't get me wrong. I've had my share of "challenging" people too. But the abundant blessings of my relationships far outweigh the burdens.

I share this not to brag but only to testify to the substantial difference the right people can make in your life. It's worth the effort to cultivate those relationships, to take risks to be transparent with trustworthy allies, and to invest in shared goals and interests with others. I know it's worth the effort because I wouldn't be here without the people in my life. I wouldn't have achieved what I've achieved. I wouldn't have the happiness I've found. I wouldn't have overcome depression without the people who stand with me, protect me, encourage me, challenge me, and make me smile.

People like my father, Bob Hodges, whose example—especially in the areas of faith and finances—continues to inspire and shape me. People like my father-in-law, Billy Hornsby, who was my best friend. In all the years I knew him, well before I married his beautiful daughter Tammy, I never saw Billy have a bad day. He made the choice to make every day a good day no matter what and chose an attitude that allowed him to have a high appreciation for life. Then there's my pastor, Larry Stockstill, who has invested in my life and instilled in me passion for purity, prayer, integrity, and evangelism. Not to mention my mentor and friend John Maxwell, who has coached me through life and ministry, encouraged me to make every moment count, and taught me how to stay in the moment.

My closest friends all pour so much into my life. Guys like Rick Bezet, who makes me laugh, and Dino Rizzo, who's always there to help me process what's in my head. Buddies such as Lee Domingue, whom I can always count on for a good meal with great conversation; Hamp Greene, who covers me in prayer; and Ken Polk, who pushes me to dream bigger dreams.

There's my family, of course, both biological and spiritual. My amazing wife and our five children, their spouses and children, our grandkids. They are the richest part of my life, and a joy unlike any other. Second only to them, my faith family at Church of the Highlands has joined me in sharing a vision that we've worked hard to realize. Together, we've obeyed God's calling to create a place where people know God, find freedom, discover purpose, and make a difference. It's an honor to serve with them.

The foundation for all these relationships is my relationship with God. There's nothing about knowing him that seems religious to me. He's my Father, my Savior, and my best Friend who never fails me. What a joy to spend time with him!

Yes, I love relationships and appreciate the vast difference they've made in my life.

And your relationships can impact you just as positively, if they haven't already.

God designed relationships to be the single greatest sustaining contributor to your health, happiness, and success. And I'm convinced that he will give all of us opportunities to have relationships that help us through the darkest times and sustain us on the other side so we don't end up right back in the cave.

There's no better place to end our journey out of the cave of depression than in the company of others!

Sidekick and Shotgun Rider

As we consider a game plan for building and fortifying healthy, life-sustaining relationships, let's return one last time to Elijah's journey out of depression. His example reminds us of the vital importance of relationships, not only with God but with other people.

You'll recall how Elijah was physically strengthened by food and sleep. He met with God and got a new perspective after listening to the

Lord's gentle whisper. God asked Elijah to express his emotions and then gave Elijah a new assignment that provided clarity about who he was and what his purpose could accomplish.

Finally moving forward out of his cave, Elijah then spent the rest of his life mentoring a protégé named Elisha, which was part of God's assignment.

> So Elijah went from there and found Elisha son of Shaphat. He was plowing with twelve yoke of oxen, and he himself was driving the twelfth pair. Elijah went up to him and threw his cloak around him. Elisha then left his oxen and ran after Elijah. "Let me kiss my father and mother goodbye," he said, "and then I will come with you."
>
> "Go back," Elijah replied. "What have I done to you?"
>
> So Elisha left him and went back. He took his yoke of oxen and slaughtered them. He burned the plowing equipment to cook the meat and gave it to the people, and they ate. Then he set out to follow Elijah and became his servant. (1 Kings 19:19–21)

After leaving the cave on Mount Horeb, we never hear about Elijah being alone again. The rest of his life is marked by the people around him, especially Elisha, who became his sidekick and shotgun rider.

Okay, those aren't the terms they probably used. But remember when you first got your driver's license and your friends would rush to be the first to call, "Shotgun!" when you drove somewhere together? They wanted to be beside you in the passenger seat and enjoy the journey with you—even if you were just cruising up the boulevard to Sonic! We all long for that kind of friend who comes alongside us on our journey through life. The kind of friend that Elijah had in Elisha.

There's one more thing we never hear about Elijah—the

death-grip of his depression. Perhaps he experienced other bouts with it, but I'd like to think that Elijah learned enough about how to overcome depression that he never again retreated into the darkness of his cave.

Elijah's life illustrates how stepping into healthy, soul-nourishing, godly relationships can sustain our overall health and help prevent emotional cave-ins. We all need others to lean on, to learn from, and to laugh with. Remember, God said it's not good for us to be alone (Genesis 2:18).

We all need others if we're going to grow.

Relationships are essential for us to bloom.

Together in Full Bloom

In a TED talk on battling depression, Johann Hari emphasized the importance of relationships and community.[1] He recalled talking with Professor John Cacioppo, considered one of the world's leading experts on loneliness. Cacioppo shared his insight that human beings no longer have to band together in tribes and groups in order to survive. In ancient times, survival depended on cooperating and collaborating in order to build shelters, to protect against predators, and to hunt and gather food. Cacioppo called this "our superpower as a species," our ability to unite interdependently. Now, we're all experiencing the fallout of disbanding from our tribes, living independently to the point of self-sufficiency.

Hari cited another conversation he had with his friend Dr. Sam Everington, a general practitioner working in a poor part of East London. Although Dr. Everington prescribed antidepressants for his patients suffering depression, he decided to try another approach after noticing how lonely and isolated most of them were. He organized a support group that met twice weekly to help people battling depression and anxiety.

At first, several participants had to overcome their social anxiety in order to even show up for the meetings. A woman named Lisa literally started throwing up because she was initially so anxious, but she ultimately found acceptance and comfort as others shared their own distress about being there. Eventually, group members decided they wanted a project so they could do more than just talk about their depression. They decided to transform an undeveloped scrap of land behind the medical clinic into a landscaped garden.

None of them had much gardening experience, so they had to do some research and talk with experts at nurseries. Soon, the group came together as a united tribe of people sharing in the creation of something new and beautiful. Lisa summed up the transformation by noting, "As the garden began to bloom, we began to bloom."

At Dr. Everington's invitation, Johann Hari visited the lush garden that had formerly been undeveloped scrubland. He was impressed by its beauty but even more taken by the truth it reflected. "So often when people feel down in this culture, we say, 'Just be yourself.' I realized, actually, what we should say to people is, 'Don't be yourself. Be us, be we. Be part of a group.'"

The treatment implemented by Dr. Everington is called "social prescribing," and its use continues to grow as its effectiveness proves itself time and again. Doctors and researchers studying social prescribing continue to accumulate evidence that it provides real and lasting recovery for those struggling with depression. Participants not only realize they're not alone with their overwhelming, painful feelings, but also create lasting relational bonds as their group pursues a joint project that gives meaning to their lives.

They realize they're no longer alone.

And they're part of a group where they belong.

Dirty Feet and Welcome Mats

Taking inventory of your closest personal relationships is also a way to take a significant step out of depression. In fact, I'd suggest that evaluating your friendships is critical to your spiritual growth and well-being. Show me your friends and I'll show you your future. "Walk with the wise and become wise, for a companion of fools suffers harm" (Proverbs 13:20).

In order to step into healthier relationships, you may need to have a hard conversation, reveal the truth about something you've kept hidden, or ask forgiveness for the pain you've caused someone close to you. Similarly, you may need to stand up to someone who's used to controlling you, enforce strong boundaries, and choose to forgive them whether or not they ask you to do so. Even if you can't sever destructive relationships with a clean break, you can at least redefine them or change what you can change in yourself.

And just so we're clear, I'm not talking about divorcing your spouse on unbiblical grounds or twisting this practice for personal advantage. Just because someone frustrates you or makes your life uncomfortable, you can't necessarily just walk away. God often uses others to reveal our blind spots and areas in which we need to follow his guidelines more closely and consistently.

But truly harmful relationships must not be allowed to continue. The ones that cause you to dread answering your phone, the ones that leave you feeling confused about your beliefs and uncertain of who you are, the ones that bombard you with criticism, deception, abuse, or pessimism. The ones that pull you away from God.

The Bible provides great clarity about which relationships to leave behind, which is any and all that hinder your relationship with God: "Do not be misled: 'Bad company corrupts good character'" (1 Corinthians 15:33). So consider the people who have access to you, the ones who influence you in person and online—including those coming through your music, movies, video games, and apps. I love what Gandhi is attributed with saying, "I will not let anyone walk through my mind with their dirty feet." I wonder how many of us have muddy thoughts because we've allowed others to trample through our minds.

Whose dirty feet have walked through your mind recently?

Maybe it's time to sweep away the grime they've left behind.

It may also be time to roll out the welcome mat for people with the potential to enhance our lives. Just as we need to quit or redefine damaging relationships, we also need to cultivate ones that give us life and strengthen our faith. We may need to risk being transparent with friends who have proven to be trustworthy. Quality relationships don't just "happen." They take time and intentionality—and we can be intentional about connecting with people who add to our lives.

This is key to our emotional health.

Part of the Pack

I often think of my friends as a wolf pack. It expresses the way we run together, do life together, and have each other's backs. We're stronger together and stronger as individuals because of our commitment to and investment in one another. We shelter and protect each other. We comfort and console each other. We encourage and uplift each other. We cry together (well, only occasionally because we're fierce, manly wolves) and we laugh a lot.

Dr. John Townsend, a Christian psychologist and bestselling coauthor of the contemporary classic *Boundaries*, calls such friends your comrades, the members of your life team. These are people who know all about you and accept you fully, but also tell you the truths you need to hear. Comrades are also fully committed to their own growth and are vulnerable with you, as they want help from you as well, in mutual improvement. There's trust, connection, and reciprocity with comrades. Experiencing community with true comrades is critical for your emotional health and safety as you move out of your cave of depression.

And comrades aren't the only close relationships we need. Coaches, as Dr. Townsend labels them, are just as vital. Coaches are mentors who teach you, challenge you, affirm you, and call you out. The best mentors see who you are as well as the fullness of your potential and lead you toward being all you can be as God created you. These coaches not only pour knowledge and wisdom into you, but they share their spirit with you as well.

Coaches and mentors differ from comrades in three distinct ways. First, they're experts in some area of common interest—leadership, parenting, ministry, physical training, or finance, for example. Second, they're not only willing to help you grow but are aware of how to help you grow. They know how to coach you to a higher level. And they are particularly effective because they're not looking for you to give back to them at the same level. Which is the third trait of a great coach: They don't need you to be a friend, fan, or buddy. They want to pour into your life because of what they have been blessed to share.

How do you find a mentor or coach? Praying and asking God is the best way to start, of course, and looking for natural opportunities with the people around you. Once you've identified someone you would like as your coach, spend some time getting to know them well enough to make sure your interests, beliefs, and values align. Then, be transparent and direct and ask them. If they agree, discuss expectations and ways you can spend time together. If not, then thank them and keep looking.

Being direct and transparent works well with anyone you want to know on a deeper, more personal level. Honesty and vulnerability usually follow when there's a clear connection or bond formed between two people. You each take off your masks and tell the truth about your lives.

This way of relating requires risk and sometimes feels uncomfortable or awkward, especially at first, but it's one of the tried and true ways to leave your cave behind forever. Because to be fully functioning we have to be fully connected and loved. And to be fully connected and loved we have to be fully known.

We're all used to wearing masks and playing roles, being what we think others need us to be in order to get what we want from them. But as the layers and motives and role playing accumulate, we get further and further away from authenticity, honesty, and transparency.

If we don't have trustworthy, godly relationships in which we can remove the layers that form our masks, we won't feel known. We won't feel safe to share who we are and what's really going on behind the polite fronts or requisite roles. Masks help us cling to denial and stay in the dark. We all harbor secrets, but you're in trouble if you're the only one who carries them.

Your secrets are the germs infecting your soul. When you tell the truth and reveal who you are, you kill the germs of pretense, pride, and protection that the enemy often uses to his advantage. Remember, God's healing process is based on confession: "Confess your sins to each other and pray for each other so that you may be healed" (James 5:16).

The enemy works hard to convince us that we must never let others see who we really are. He whispers that if we reveal our hearts, then others will hurt us, exploit us, mock us, reject us, and abandon us. Believing his lies, we create walls and develop defenses to protect the tender, fragile heart inside. But over time, those walls and defenses get thicker and harder until we've built a prison for ourselves. We sentence ourselves to the solitary confinement of our caves and hide in the dark from the source of light that can liberate us.

You know now, however, it doesn't have to be this way.

You're standing at the mouth of your cave.

You've heard God's voice and know he has a new mission for you.

You're taking steps into the light.

Where you realize you're not alone.

Ransomed and Rescued

Toward the end of his life, Elijah tried to go solo again. He basically kept telling Elisha, "Stay here while I go on to this place or that city." But Elisha wouldn't leave him. Unlike the unnamed servant from the beginning of the story whom Elijah left behind, Elisha refused to leave, even when commanded to do so. Elisha was a true friend, the kind who sticks closer than a brother. He represents the kind of people we all need in our lives to help us avoid isolation and depression.

The joy of being part of a godly community cannot be measured. And if you want to step into this kind of authentic, joyful belonging, focus on being the kind of friend you want to have. You reap what you sow, and nowhere does this reveal itself to be truer than in your relationships. Elijah spent the rest of his life mentoring Elisha, and Elisha valued all his mentor had poured into him: "Elijah said to Elisha, 'Tell me, what can I do for you before I am taken from you?' 'Let me inherit a double portion of your spirit,' Elisha replied" (2 Kings 2:9).

This passing of the torch would be the final act of Elijah's life. He had invested fully in someone else's life so that his wisdom, experience, and victories would form an eternal legacy. As Elijah focused on investing in his spiritual son, Elisha, he found renewed purpose and joy. To our knowledge, Elijah never battled depression again.

As I survey Elijah's journey out of the cave, I believe this bond with Elisha, the gift of making a difference in the life of another person, brought light to both their souls. Elijah's example reveals the prescription for you and me as well. Our lives are meant to be shared, invested, and enjoyed with other people.

This is the heart of what our lives are really all about—loving others.

Which is why the devil works so hard to push us toward our caves of depression.

If he can get us to withdraw into the darkness, believing his lies that we're alone and always will be, our cave becomes a prison of our own making.

But God has given us the tools we need to defeat depression and step forward into the light. In the light we can see clearly who God made us to be and what he designed us to do. We can experience the joy of moving forward, trusting him each step of the way as we clasp the hands of others traveling alongside us.

You are not alone, my friend. And you no longer have to hide in a cave of fear, anxiety, stress, anger, and uncertainty. God meets you there. He gives you rest for your soul and nourishment for your body. He whispers his love to you and gives you a new assignment.

It's time to assess your relationships and commit to your Elisha and the others God brings across your path. As you experience the exhilaration of moving into a new season of life, I can think of no better way to close our journey together through these pages than to offer a prayer. Use this prayer as kindling to ignite your own flame of praise and worship. Talk to the Lord and listen to his response.

You never have to go back to your cave again.

To God be the glory!

Dear Lord,

   God of heaven and earth, of Elijah and Elisha, thank you for always meeting me in the darkness of my depression.

In the days, weeks, and months ahead, remind me of your truth and the lessons I've learned in these pages. Give me a fresh perspective—your perspective—on my life, on my relationships, and on my purpose.

Show me the way, Lord, out of the cave where I've spent far too much time feeling lonely and alone. I'm trusting you for every step forward.

As I walk into the light of my new life, I know all the glory, honor, and praise belong to you! Thank you for loving me enough to ransom me from my sins and to rescue me from my cave. Glory to you, O Lord! In Jesus' name I pray, amen.

Acknowledgments

To all my family and friends who offered support, encouragement, and assistance on this project, I appreciate you more than you'll ever know. I'm especially grateful for:

My writer, Dudley Delffs: Thank you for being my writing partner for more than eight years. Once again, you gave your heart and soul into making my sentences make sense.

My agent, Matt Yates: Thank you for the encouragement, insight, and wisdom you provided throughout this entire process. I'm so grateful for your counsel and support.

My team at Nelson Books, Jessica Wong, Christine Anderson, and Janene MacIvor: Thank you for all of your hard work on this project. You make me better in every way.

My friend, Lysa Terkeurst: Thank you for helping me become a better writer. Your training, feedback, and suggestions have taught me so much.

My book team at Highlands, Kellen Coldiron, Katie Vogel, Chris Hanna, Matt Minor, Gina Cox, and Michael Hodges: Thank you for your invaluable contributions. You continue to be such a blessing to my life and ministry.

My friend, John Maxwell: Thank you for being my mentor and friend. You add so much value to every part of my life. I love doing life and ministry together.

My executive assistant, Katy Hodges: Thank you for serving me so well. You are a gift from God.

My wife, Tammy: Thank you for standing with me side by side for more than thirty-four years. I love you more than words can express.

My LORD and Savior, Jesus Christ: Thank you for choosing me. I truly don't deserve it. It is my honor to serve You.

Stepping into the Truth
of God's Word

Bible Verses for Hope and Comfort
When You Are Depressed

Read and pray these verses to remind your soul of the truth of who God is. Because of his character, goodness, and love, you are empowered to step out of your cave.

- "For I know the plans I have for you," declares the LORD, "plans to prosper you and not to harm you, plans to give you hope and a future." (Jeremiah 29:11)

    Because God has your best in mind, you can trust him with your future. He has a plan for you, even if your current circumstances make it difficult to see.

- From the end of the earth I will cry to You, when my heart is overwhelmed; Lead me to the rock that is higher than I. (Psalm 61:2 NKJV)

  Because God is your Rock, you have a solid, safe place to go when you are overwhelmed. He will steady your heart and mind.

- Yet this I call to mind and therefore I have hope: Because of the LORD's great love we are not consumed, for his compassions never fail. They are new every morning; great is your faithfulness. (Lamentations 3:21–23)

  Because God is faithful, you can trust him to carry you through this day. He has new strength and new compassion for you every day.

- Finally, brothers and sisters, whatever is true, whatever is noble, whatever is right, whatever is pure, whatever is lovely, whatever is admirable—if anything is excellent or praiseworthy—think about such things. Whatever you have learned or received or heard from me, or seen in me—put it into practice. And the God of peace will be with you. (Philippians 4:8–9).

  Because Jesus is the Prince of Peace, you have access to peace in this moment. He can help you control your thoughts. Keep your mind set on things that are good, encouraging, beautiful, and true, and rest in the peace of God.

- The LORD himself goes before you and will be with you; he will never leave you nor forsake you. Do not be afraid; do not be discouraged. (Deuteronomy 31:8)

  Because God is with you, you are never alone. He will never leave you in your pain. He is right beside you.

- The righteous cry out, and the LORD hears them; he delivers them from all their troubles. (Psalm 34:17)

  Because God hears you, you can trust that he knows what you need.

- If your heart is broken, you'll find GOD right there; if you're kicked in the gut, he'll help you catch your breath. (Psalm 34:18 THE MESSAGE)

  Because God cares about your pain, he pays attention to you. Cry out to him; he is close and eager to help you.

- I waited patiently for the LORD to help me, and he turned to me and heard my cry. He lifted me out of the pit of despair, out of the mud and the mire. He set my feet on solid ground and steadied me as I walked along. He has given me a new song to sing, a hymn of praise to our God. Many will see what he has done and be amazed. They will put their trust in the LORD. (Psalm 40:1–3 NLT)

  Because Jesus came for you to have a full life, he will not leave you where you are. He will lift you out of this pit, set your feet on solid ground, steady you, and give you a new reason to praise him. Your testimony from this season of your life will bring God glory!

- Why are you down in the dumps, dear soul? Why are you crying the blues? Fix my eyes on God—soon I'll be praising again. He puts a smile on my face. He's my God. (Psalm 42:11 THE MESSAGE)

  Because God is good, he is worthy of praise! As you focus on who he is and what he has done for you, he will give you joy.

- Cast all your anxiety on him because he cares for you. (1 Peter 5:7)

  Because God cares for you, he wants you to give him your problems. Lay your worries and fears at his feet, and trust him to take care of them.

- "I've told you all this so that trusting me, you will be unshakable and assured, deeply at peace. In this godless world you will continue to experience difficulties. But take heart! I've conquered the world." (John 16:33 THE MESSAGE)

Because Jesus has conquered the world, nothing is too difficult for him. There is nothing you face that he has not overcome. He shares that victory with you.

- I am convinced that nothing can ever separate us from God's love. Neither death nor life, neither angels nor demons, neither our fears for today nor our worries about tomorrow—not even the powers of hell can separate us from God's love. No power in the sky above or in the earth below—indeed, nothing in all creation will ever be able to separate us from the love of God that is revealed in Christ Jesus our Lord. (Romans 8:38–39 NLT)

  Because God's love for you is unfailing, nothing you think or do can make him stop loving you.

- Friends, when life gets really difficult, don't jump to the conclusion that God isn't on the job. Instead, be glad that you are in the very thick of what Christ experienced. This is a spiritual refining process, with glory just around the corner. (1 Peter 4:12–13 THE MESSAGE)

  Because Jesus knows how you feel, you have an advocate. He experienced everything you're experiencing. He is working in your life, and he will not let these days be wasted.

- "Don't panic. I'm with you. There's no need to fear for I'm your God. I'll give you strength. I'll help you. I'll hold you steady, keep a firm grip on you." (Isaiah 41:10 THE MESSAGE)

  Because God is holding you steady, you do not have to be afraid. He will not let you go.

Let these truths sink into your soul, and let God's goodness and posture toward you give you boldness to step out of your cave.

Spiritual Warfare Prayers

The prayers offered in the state of dryness
are those which please Him best.
—C. S. LEWIS

Prayer for Clarity and Discernment

EPHESIANS 6:12; ACTS 26:18

God, I recognize that my struggles today aren't against the people or circumstances around me, but against the enemy. Please help me see how the enemy is lying to me. Help me recognize his lies, take them captive, and make all of my thoughts obedient to the truth of your Word. *[List any specific areas in which you have believed a lie that needs to be replaced with God's truth.]*

While the enemy wants to destroy me, I know that you came to give me life to the fullest. I speak the name of Jesus over my life and declare that no weapon formed against me will prosper. I don't have to fear the enemy because the One who is in me is greater than the one who is in the world.

The Armor of God

EPHESIANS 6:10–17

Acknowledge that you're in a spiritual battle. Then, claim the protection God has given you by praying through the different pieces of armor described in Ephesians 6.

Lord, I declare this day that nothing can separate me from the love of Christ and the place I have in your kingdom. I wear your righteousness today against all condemnation and corruption. Cover me with your holiness and purity—defend me from all attacks against my heart.

I put on the belt of truth. I choose a lifestyle of honesty and integrity. Expose the lies I have believed and show me your truth today. I choose to live for the gospel in every moment.

Show me where you are working and lead me to it. Give me strength to walk daily with you. I believe that you are powerful against every lie and attack of the enemy, and I receive and claim your power in my life. Nothing is coming today that can overcome me because you are with me.

Holy Spirit, show me the truths of the Word of God that I will need to counter the traps of the enemy. Bring those scriptures to mind today. I agree to walk in step with you in everything as my spirit communes with you in prayer throughout the day.

The Weapons of Warfare

2 CORINTHIANS 10:4–5

You have authority to command anything that comes against the truth of God and his Word to bow to the name of Jesus. Take a bold stand, praying specifically and confidently through God's power and his Spirit.

Father, your Word says that no weapon formed against me will prosper (Isaiah 54:17), and I declare it in Jesus' name. Your Word says that trouble will not arise a second time (Nahum 1:9). I declare in Jesus' name that Satan cannot make trouble for me again as he has in the past. I declare in the name of Jesus that all these prayers are answered and taken care of by trusting you.

I stand on your Word. The enemy is driven out from me—from my home, workplace, church family, children, and loved ones. I declare that he is not able to stand against me. No weapon formed against me will prosper because the Spirit of the Lord is with me, protecting me.

I declare these truths in the name of Jesus. Anything that comes against me or my family that is not in line with the truth and will of God, I command to bow to the powerful name of Jesus.

Father God, I give you all of my thanksgiving, praise, glory, honor, and worship. Thank you for loving me, making me clean, and giving me purpose.

Protection Prayer

2 THESSALONIANS 3:3; 2 CORINTHIANS 6:14–7:1, 10:3–5; ROMANS 12:1–2

We often worry about our safety and protection. When we feel this way, we can immediately come to God in prayer, pouring out our hearts to him, and battling in the heavenlies by asking for and claiming protection for ourselves and our families in Jesus' name. The Lord is faithful, and he will strengthen you and protect you from the evil one.

God, I bow in worship to praise you. Thank you for making a way for me through your Son, Jesus. I surrender myself to you completely in every area of my life. I submit myself to the true and living God and refuse to allow the enemy any involvement in my life. I choose to be transformed by the renewing of my mind. I reject every thought that tries to compete against the knowledge of Christ. I thank you for a sound mind, the mind of Christ.

Today and every day, I ask for protection for my family and loved ones—all immediate family members, relatives, friends, acquaintances, and myself. I ask for protection during all our travels. I ask you to watch over our financial security, possessions, health, and safety. *[Be specific here.]*

All that I have is yours, and I declare that Satan cannot touch me or anything you have given me. I rebuke the enemy and tell him to bow to the blood of Jesus that covers me and my family. He will not take what you have given us, and we are protected and provided for by you, God, and you alone.

Praying for Loved Ones
Who Are Depressed

The following prayers are ones prayed by my wife, Tammy, when I am battling depression. She prays the first prayer for me and the second prayer for herself. Use them as models for your own prayers when walking through depression with loved ones.

Praying for Others Who Are Depressed

TAMMY'S PRAYER FOR CHRIS

Father, I come to you now in the name of Jesus for Chris. You know where he is in his soul, mind, and spirit right now, and he needs your help. I ask you, Holy Spirit, to move inside of him—body, soul, and spirit—to bring into alignment in every physical issue that is working against him, every thought that is plaguing his mind, and every evil spirit that is attacking him. Please move in close to him and bring him comfort in every way.

The Word of God says that the Holy Spirit helps us in our weakness. Lord, Chris needs your help now. I pray that every lie the enemy is telling him will be exposed by the truth. I bind every thought that comes from the evil one, and I ask that Chris will recognize your voice only. I ask that you will bring healing to Chris's mind. I thank you, Jesus, that you took the stripes on your back for our healing. Lead us to help for complete physical health.

Lord, I pray that you will send people to Chris to encourage him. I pray that they will speak life to him and dispel every bit of darkness. I bind negative words off of him. Lord, I pray that as Chris seeks you, your peace will flood in and guard his heart and mind. Please, through your Holy Spirit, help him focus on what is true, noble, right, pure, lovely, admirable, excellent, and praiseworthy. In Jesus' name, amen.

When Praying for Yourself as You Walk with Others Suffering Depression

TAMMY'S PRAYER FOR HERSELF

Lord, I come to you for help. I am battling thoughts and feelings that have brought darkness and heaviness. Please take this from me. Your Word says that if I come to you with this in prayer, your peace will guard my heart and mind. Please shed light on lies I have believed. Please free me from every evil attack of the enemy. Please bring hope, joy, and light back into my life. Please heal my soul, body, and spirit. Help me believe and trust that with you all things are possible. Forgive me in my doubt and help me supernaturally. Thank you, Jesus, that you are at God's right hand interceding for me. I am thankful that nothing can separate me from your love. Please set me free. I confess that I will be more than a conqueror in all of this. In Jesus' name, amen.

Suicide Prevention

If you have any doubt in your mind about your will to live, or if you are suicidal or thinking of hurting yourself or others, please call 988 to reach the National Suicide Prevention Hotline. In the US, you can also call the National Suicide Prevention Lifeline, available twenty-four hours a day at 800-273-8255 or text HOME to 741741 to reach the Crisis Text Line (in Canada call 833-456-4566).

Notes

Introduction

1. Brandi Koski, "Depression: Facts, Statistics, and You," Healthline, June 3, 2020, https://www.healthline.com/health/depression/facts -statistics-infographic#7.

2. Keith Oatley, "Slings and Arrows: Depression and Life Events," *The Psychologist* 20, no. 4 (April 2007):228–231. https://thepsychologist. bps.org.uk/volume-20/edition-4/slings-and-arrows-depression-and -life-events, accessed September 24, 2020.

Chapter 2: What You Might Not Know About Depression

1. Adapted from Twitter, https://twitter.com/hashtag/depressionfeelslike ?src=hashtag_click; Instagram, https://www.instagram.com/explore /tags/depressionfeelslike/?hl=en; and "Describing Depression to Those Who've Never Had It," Blurt, July 8, 2016, https://www.blurtitout.org /2016/07/08/describing-depression-whove-never/.

2. Pat Reynolds, "10 Phrases You Never Knew Came from Sailing," American Sailing Association, August 12, 2015. https://asa.com/news /2015/08/12/phrases-from-sailing/.

3. Mandalit Del Barco, "Sacred, Sad and Salacious: With Many Meanings, What Is True Blue?" *All Things Considered* (NPR), November 12, 2014. https://www.npr.org/2014/11/12/363549525 /sacred-sad-and-salacious-with-many-meanings-what-is-true-blue#.

4. "What Causes Depression?," Harvard Health Publishing, June 24, 2019, https://www.health.harvard.edu/mind-and-mood/what-causes -depression.

5. Johann Hari, *Lost Connections: Why You're Depressed and How to Find Hope* (London: Bloomsbury Publishing, 2018), 71–73.

6. Sharifa Z. Williams, Grace C. Chung, and Peter A. Muennig, "Undiagnosed Depression: A Community Diagnosis," *SSM Popul Health* 3 (July 28, 2017):633-638. DOI: 10.10.16/j.ssmph.2017.07.012. https://www.ncbi.nlm.nih.gov/pmc/articles/PMC5769115/.

Chapter 4: Life Imbalance

1. Dainius Pūras, "Depression: Let's Talk About How We Address Mental Health," Office of the United Nations High Commissioner for Human Rights, April 7, 2017, http://www.ohchr.org/EN/NewsEvents /Pages/DisplayNews.aspx?NewsID=21480&LangID=E.

2. Stephen S. Ilardi, PhD, *The Depression Cure: The Six-Step Program to Beat Depression Without Drugs* (Cambridge, MA: De Capo Press, 2009), 253.

3. George W. Crane, quoted in David Schwartz, *The Magic of Thinking Big* (New York: Touchstone/Simon & Schuster, 2015), 68.

4. Often attributed to Frankl, this quotation is now believed to have been used by Stephen R. Covey to summarize Frankl's view. See https://www .univie.ac.at/logotherapy/quote_stimulus.html, accessed November 20, 2020.

Chapter 5: Scrolling Away My Peace

1. Quoted in Dimitrios Tsatiris, "The #1 Misconception About Success: How to Avoid This Common Trap," *Psychology Today* (November 18, 2020).

2. "ScreenTime: Diane Sawyer Reporting; Two-hour ABC News Special, Challenges Families to Rethink Technology Consumption," ABC7 News, May 2, 2019, https://abc7news.com/technology/abc-special -challenges-families-to-rethink-screen-time/5282005/.

3. Nicole Nguyen, "Doomscrolling: Why We Just Can't Look Away," *Wall Street Journal*, June 7, 2020, https://www.wsj.com/articles/doom scrolling-why-we-just-cant-look-away-11591522200?mod=cxrecs_join #cxrecs_s.

4. The Social Dilemma (website). NetFlix Documentary, 2020. https://www.thesocialdilemma.com/.

5. Devika Girish, "'The Social Dilemma' Review: Unplug and Run," *The New York Times*, September 9, 2020, retrieved September 17, 2020, https://en.wikipedia.org/wiki/Anna_Lembke from https://www.thesocialdilemma.com/.

6. Nicole Nguyen, "Doomscrolling."

CHAPTER 6: CHEWING THE CUD

1. Ilardi, *The Depression Cure*, 92.

2. Brian L. Alderman, et al. "Rumination in Major Depressive Disorder Is Associated with Impaired Neural Activation During Conflict Monitoring," *Frontiers in Human Neuroscience* 9 (May 12, 2015):269, DOI:10.3389/fnhum.2015.00269.https://www.ncbi.nlm.nih.gov/pmc/articles/PMC4428129/, accessed November 20, 2020.

3. Paraphrased from John Maxwell, *Thinking for a Change: Eleven Ways Highly Successful People Approach Life and Work* (New York: Center Street, 2005), 7.

4. Craig Groeschel, *Soul Detox: Clean Living in a Contaminated World* (Grand Rapids, MI: Zondervan, 2012), 65.

CHAPTER 7: SOCIAL DISTANCING

1. John T. Cacioppo, Louise C. Hawkley, "Perceived Social Isolation and Cognition," *Trends in Cognitive Science* 10, October 13, 2009, https://www.ncbi.nlm.nih.gov/pmc/articles/PMC2752489/.

2. Adapted from Appendix 2 in *Gospel Coach: Shepherding Leaders to Glorify God* by Scott Thomas and Tom Wood (Grand Rapids, MI: Zondervan, 2012).

CHAPTER 8: RAINY DAYS AND MONDAYS

1. David Webb, "Carl Rogers," All-About-Psychology.com, 2008–2020, https://www.all-about-psychology.com/carl_rogers.html, accessed November 20, 2020.

2. "Philippians: A Verse-by-Verse Exegetical Commentary on the Greek New Testament" (Lectionarystudies.com), http://www.lectionarystudies.com/studyn/introphil.html, accessed November 20, 2020.

CHAPTER 9: THE UNSEEN ENEMY

1. C. S. Lewis, *The Screwtape Letters*, Reprint Edition, (San Francisco, CA: HarperOne, 2015), 4.
2. Barna Group, "Most American Christians Do Not Believe That Satan or the Holy Spirit Exist," Barna Group Ltd., April 13, 2009, https://www .barna.com/research/most-american-christians-do-not-believe-that-satan -or-the-holy-spirit-exist/.

CHAPTER 10: STEPPING INTO A NEEDED RECOVERY

1. Tony Merida, *Exalting Jesus in 1 & 2 Kings*, Christ-Centered Exposition Commentary (Nashville, TN: Holman Reference, 2015), 138–139.
2. Fred R. Shapiro, "Who Wrote the Serenity Prayer?" *The Chronicle of Higher Education* 60, no. 33 (April 28, 2014), https://www.chronicle.com /article/who-wrote-the-serenity-prayer/, accessed November 20, 2020.

CHAPTER 11: STEPPING INTO A GOD ENCOUNTER

1. For example, Moses twice spent forty days on Mount Sinai (Exodus 24:18; 34:28), the prophet Jonah spent forty days warning Nineveh to repent (Jonah 3:4), and Jesus spent forty days in the desert before beginning his public ministry (Matthew 4:1–2).

CHAPTER 12: STEPPING INTO A TRUE IDENTITY

1. Summary of Marina Chapman, *The Girl with No Name: The Incredible Story of a Child Raised by Monkeys*, Illustrated Edition (New York: Pegasus Books, 2014).
2. Wency Leung, "Maria Chapman's Wild Tale of a Feral Childhood Sparks Skepticism," *The Globe and Mail*, May 2, 2013, https://www .theglobeandmail.com/life/relationships/marina-chapmans-wild-tale -of-a-feral-childhood-sparks-skepticism/article11690193/.

CHAPTER 13: STEPPING INTO A NEW ASSIGNMENT

1. Biographical details of Viktor Frankl's life are taken from the website of the Viktor Frankl Institute, https://www.viktorfrankl.org/biography .html.
2. Viktor Frankl Institute, https://www.viktorfrankl.org/biography.html.

3. Viktor E. Frankl, *Man's Search for Meaning* (Boston: Beacon Press, 2006), 14.

4. Johann Hari, *Lost Connections*, 193–198.

Chapter 14: Stepping into Relational Strength

1. The following stories are summarized from Johann Hari, "This Could Be Why You're Depressed or Anxious," TEDSummit 2019, https://www.ted.com/talks/johann_hari_this_could_be_why_you_re_depressed_or_anxious?language=en#t-53632.

About the Author

Chris Hodges, founding and senior pastor of Church of the Highlands, is known for his relevant teaching style and his passion for raising up global leaders to fulfill the Great Commission. Chris and his wife, Tammy, have five children and six grandchildren and live in Birmingham, Alabama, where Church of the Highlands began in 2001.

Under his leadership, Church of the Highlands offers more than sixty worship services each weekend at twenty-three campuses with more than sixty thousand people attending weekly. With a focus on helping people realize the spiritual journey that God has for them, Chris leads people to know God, find freedom, discover purpose, and make a difference.

Chris cofounded the Association of Related Churches (ARC at arcchurches.com) in 2001, which trains more than one thousand church planters every year and gives more than $7 million annually to church planters. To date, ARC has planted more than nine hundred churches all across the USA (now averaging more than one hundred new churches every year).

Chris also founded a coaching network called Grow (growleader.com) to help churches reach their full growth potential. Each year more than seven thousand pastors attend sold-out conferences and roundtables in America, Europe, Australia, and Asia led by Chris and his team. These events train pastors and leaders in a simple yet systematic model based on his bestselling books *What's Next?* and *Fresh Air*. Thousands of churches now use this model and continue to break growth barriers.

As chancellor of Highlands College (highlandscollege.com), an accredited two-year ministry training college that gives students a chance to receive hands-on ministry training in a healthy college environment, Chris is committed to placing leaders of character into the harvest field. Students are currently being developed in areas such as pastoral leadership, student ministry, worship, and creative arts.

Chris also serves on the board of directors of EQUIP, a global leadership training organization founded by John Maxwell. EQUIP has trained more than 6 million leaders in 196 countries of the world.

Chris's educational background includes a BA in management from Colorado Christian University and a master of ministry from Southwestern Christian University.

Chris's other books include *The Daniel Dilemma* and *Four Cups*.

New Video Study for Your Church or Small Group

If you've enjoyed this book, now you can go deeper with the companion video Bible study!

In this five-session video Bible study, bestselling author and pastor Chris Hodges draws on the story of Elijah to show no matter how powerful, accomplished, or successful we may be, we can all still succumb to fear, doubt, despair, and hopelessness. Like Elijah, we can become overcomers and press on to God-inspired victory.

Study Guide
9780310117513

DVD with
Free Streaming Access
9780310117537

Available now at your favorite bookstore,
or streaming video on StudyGateway.com.